COMMUNITY
MOSAIC

COMMUNITY MOSAIC

Competencies for Multicultural Ministry

by
SUSAN B. CAROLE

Cover design: J.R. Caines
Interior design: Sharon Page

CONTENTS
▼▲▼

FOREWORD
▼▲▼

The United States and Canada are two of the most culturally and linguistically diverse countries in the world. This diversity has been shaped by waves of people from different countries around the world who have immigrated to take up residency in these two North American nations. The United States and Canada are frequently referred to as countries of immigrants. The USA/ Canada Region is a fertile mission field, and local churches have a great opportunity to reach people from all over the world in their communities.

As the world has moved into the United States and Canada, the landscape of these societies has become increasingly multicultural and multilingual. The rising tide of multiculturalism characterizes the present and future of most institutions in U.S. and Canadian society, and the church needs to be attuned to this new reality.

The sons and daughters of the first generation of immigrants comprise a rapidly growing demographic that can be reached in a multicultural congregation setting since they are so familiar with the multicultural context in their schools, neighborhoods, workplaces, and social gatherings, and they prefer the English language for communication.

Community Mosaic: Competencies for Multicultural Ministry by Dr. Susan B. Carole provides a road map for beginning conversations relative to establishing new multicultural congregations or strengthening existing ones. Dr. Carole introduces biblical, theological, sociological, and practical models to guide implementation of concepts relating to this type of congregation.

The material is presented as a three-step process: *Awareness*—recognizing the cultural situation and the need for missional response. *Acknowledgment*—accepting cultural diversity and acquiring skills to build cross-cultural relationships. *Discernment*—identifying best practices for unique ministry contexts.

At the end of each chapter are questions that can serve as reflection for the reader, or for group study, or church committee dialogue on the dynamics of the multicultural congregation.

Thank you to Dr. Carole and to those who contributed to this valuable discussion on *being* and *doing* ministry in a multicultural congregation. Special appreciation to Rev. Junior Sorzano, Multicultural Congregations facilitator, for his leadership and input with this project. Also to Jeanette Littleton for her editing and attention to final details of publishing. May we continue on with the mission, "To Make Christlike Disciples in the Nations."

—Dr. Roberto Hodgson, Multicultural Ministries Director

PREFACE

▼▲▼

In the mid 1600s Christianity in Europe began to be concerned with survival. The church would survive, but probably not in the way the Europeans would have imagined. Colonial expansion into Latin America started and, with it, the spread of Christianity. In Latin America the church found new strongholds and again began to thrive. Now, centuries later, the expansion of the global south is moving north.

What we saw in Latin America also emerged in Africa. Early in the last century only 10 percent of Africa would claim Christianity. Today over 50 percent of Africa is Christian, and if you were to compare the population growth in Latin America with Africa, by 2050, Africa wins. By the year 2050 one-third of all Christians in the world will be from Africa. In Nigeria alone it is estimated that between 170 and 180 million people will be Christian.[1] Philip Jenkins tells us that Christianity is "a religion that began in ancient Africa and in our lifetime, has chosen to go home."[2] Every denomination is in transition because of the influence of Africa on Christianity.

The reality is that we see the global south moving north on a daily basis, and the implications for Christianity are huge. The demographics of the United States are shifting at a rapid rate. The study *The Next America* identifies "the new us." While in 1960 the United States was 85 percent white, by 2060 there will be a dramatic shift with only 43 percent of the population being white or Anglo. More than 40 million immigrants have arrived in the United States since 1965 with one-half Hispanic and one-third Asian. Immigrants are projected to make up 37 percent of the United States population by 2050, the highest share in U.S. history. "We've always been a nation of settlers and immigrants. In this regard, the middle of the 20th century wasn't the norm, it was the outlier."[3] The postwar and baby-boomer era was actually not the norm for America. The new landscape we face today is actually a return to a period of time when immigration and all of its blessings and challenges were major factors in North American life and Christianity.

The result is that we can no longer continue ministering in the ways that we have in the past and then simply try to add a global perspective. Instead, our overall perspective must be global, and as the African continent continues to be impacted with population growth, we must recognize that more people will emigrate. Already, today, 60,000 Nigerians are living in Houston, Texas, who have brought with them their faith and culture. Jenkins tells us, "The global church is here but the extent to which this is true may pass people by."[4] Are we noticing the changes, and are we willing to adapt the ways in which we have always done things to embrace the future, which God is already preparing?

At a recent meeting of evangelical leaders, Dr. Joseph Castleberry, president of Northwest University, spoke of the intentionality of the Assembly of God Church to increase diversity. They began to note the demographic changes in the 1980s and 1990s and made adjustments. As a result, today 40 percent of their North American churches are Hispanic. A report from the Association of Theological Schools (ATS) tells us, "Non-white and non-North American students now represent 40 percent of all students, compared to 30 percent a decade ago. At this rate, by 2025 the North American white majority will be a minority in ATS member schools."[5] This is the face of the new North America, and it should be the face of the church if we are going to be relevant and have a voice.

This beautiful new mosaic of a future is not to be feared, but, rather, to be embraced as a gift from God. Just as Christianity thought it was struggling in the mid 1600s, God was already at work. Today, God is at work in new and exciting ways, and we are simply invited to participate in this movement of God's Holy Spirit. How we do that can be a challenge, but there are those who are already providing road maps for possibilities and we can learn from them. Let's take some time to examine the ways in which God is already at work, and then outline our own intentional pathways to become a part of the tapestry of the future.

—Carla Sunberg
General Superintendent, Church of the Nazarene

ACKNOWLEDGMENTS
▼▲▼

Learning and writing about the growing edge of multicultural ministry has been an exciting journey for me. Hearing the stories of what God is doing in local churches across North America has inspired and challenged me to develop more welcoming ministry practices. This handbook for Nazarene multicultural local church ministry was inspired by the USA/Canada Multicultural Ministries leadership team, spearheaded by Dr. Roberto Hodgson and facilitated by Rev. Junior Sorzano. I am grateful to them for the opportunity to participate in this project alongside pastors and practitioners in the field of multiculturalism. Together, we offer *Community Mosaic*, a "Multicultural Congregations 101" and introduction to what is rapidly becoming a substantial field in the area of practical theology. It is a special privilege for me to be a part of this exciting dimension of the Spirit's movement in North America.

I am especially grateful to those Nazarene experts who have generously shared their insights and experiences to make this handbook a helpful resource. I have learned from them, as I hope the reader will. This is indeed marvelous to belong to a church that maintains a sharp growing edge, that demonstrates the power of transformative grace by continually moving forward into new missional endeavor, that embraces change because God empowers. A lifelong Nazarene, I have been privileged to serve in the Caribbean, West Africa, Canada, and now in the United States. All along the way, I've shared life and ministry with godly, committed Nazarenes who have demonstrated the "all in" passion for Christ that embodies the holiness message.

And I am grateful for every pastor who, by love and faithfulness, advances God's mission one person at a time. I am grateful to belong in the collegiate of Nazarene pastors, knowing that our labor is not in vain; for the Lord of the harvest, the Lord of the battle, is our very own Jesus, whom we preach, serve, and love. Thank you for doing what you do, pastor. Thank you for being faithful, growing, and loving. My prayer is that something you read in this book will encourage you, sharpen your vision, and ignite your passion for the open door that God has set before us here in North America.

—Susan Carole

CONTRIBUTORS

▼▲▼

This book is a collaborative effort, and credit must be given to these fine people for their substantial contribution:

Rev. Junior Sorzano, USA/Canada Multicultural Congregations Facilitator

Dr. Joe Knight, President, 4ETHNE Ministries

Dr. Roberto Hodgson, Director, Multicultural Ministries, USA/Canada Region

Dr. Oliver Philips, Lead Connector, Lake Como Connexions

Dr. Jerry Appleby, Consultant, LiveCOMPASSION

Dr. Bill Selvidge, Associate Professor of Intercultural Studies, Nazarene Theological Seminary

Rev. James Heyward, Senior Pastor, Annandale Calvary Church of the Nazarene

Rev. Kevin McGinnis, Senior Pastor, Mosaic Church of the Nazarene

Rev. Lynn Nichols, Senior Pastor, Northside Church of the Nazarene

Dr. Tom Nees, former Director of the USA/Canada Region

INTRODUCTION
▼▲▼

I was thrown into multicultural ministry before we had a name for it! Now, I look back and think, "Oh, so that's what we were doing! Wow! Who knew?" I look back and realize that for most of my life, I've been in ministry in multicultural contexts. I didn't know I had to learn how to do this. I just muddled through, unaware of the mistakes I was making along the way.

I still make mistakes—I miss social cues, I communicate in ways that puzzle my peers and my people. But now I know that I don't know. This means I can keep learning, and, hopefully, get better at sharing life, love, and ministry with all kinds of people. I invite you, fellow pastor, to join me on this adventure.

I hope that, like me, you will find fresh perspectives for ministry as you journey through this book. *Community Mosaic* was born out of a desire to help us shape multicultural ministry for Nazarene local churches. Whether you are already engaged in multicultural ministry, or you'd like to but don't know how to begin—whatever your present ministry space, read on.

Here's why:

- We need to come to terms with the rapid and increasing influx of immigrants from almost every continent in the world. The global mission is here.
- Multicultural ministry is not an end in itself; it is an expression of who we are—a missional people.

These two intersecting realities inform congregational life here and now:

- We are committed to pressing past cultural differences to connect with all kinds of people in redemptive ways—all kinds of people, people who are unlike us.

- The present opportunity is to know and love people who have been displaced, have lost all that is familiar, and need a place to belong. Your church and mine can become this place of belonging.
- Local churches that welcome all kinds of people end up reflecting the sociocultural mosaic of their communities.

How do I, from where I serve (in Southern California, pastoring a local church in San Bernardino), speak to my ministry partner in Vancouver, Toronto, Cleveland, Garden City, Abilene, or Phoenix? This was the daunting question I asked when first I began the journey of writing this book.

Every ministry context is unique. The challenge, social dynamic, and yes, the Spirit's moving, cannot be replicated. Just like families; no two are alike.

But, just like families, local churches share common rituals, conversations, and principles. We are doing Christian community along the same lines, but in unique contexts. By sharing experiences and insights in a book of this kind, we learn from each other and we learn together.

In reading this book, you will find affirmation for what you're already doing. You will also encounter new and challenging ideas; something new to think about. Process, reshape, and apply these insights where you are. Make them your own.

The following chapters are organized in three sections that reflect the three-step process of becoming multicultural:

Awareness—recognizing the cultural situation and the need for missional response.

Acknowledgment—accepting cultural diversity and acquiring skills to build cross-cultural relationships.

Discernment—identifying best practices for unique ministry contexts.

Awareness

Section 1 raises awareness of:
- Ethnic diversity as a sociological reality
- Biblical principles for multicultural ministry
- Wesleyan foundations for multicultural ministry

Section 1 answers the why question: *Why multicultural ministry?*

Chapter 1 explores ethnic diversity, a rapidly developing North American phenomenon, an unprecedented missional opportunity to disciple the nations here and now. This mass migration is a mosaic of stories—stories of displaced families, their griefs and gifts, their fears and hopes—waiting to be discovered and appreciated. We can come alongside immigrant families, walk with them as they navigate the unknown, and help them feel at home in our communities, in our churches.

Chapter 2 takes us to the beginning—Genesis—where we see that diversity expresses God's creativity and God's plan for human community. Diversity, we shall see, is not a problem to be solved but a reality to be understood and embraced, a part of God's good creation.

Chapter 3 is about another beginning—the church, the new creation—where we see implicit transcendence of sociocultural distinctions. The gospel is for everyone. The church is for everyone. Love has the power to bring together all kinds of people. That's the truth, and the New Testament church determinedly embraced and practiced this truth. In both Old and New Testaments, we find unequivocal biblical warrant for the multicultural project. We can express the biblical mandate in simple terms: All people are of intrinsic worth because each one is created in the image of God and loved by God.

In chapter 4 we look at the shape of authentic Wesleyan response to sociocultural diversity. Prevenient grace, holy love, Spirit-driven transformation—these theological foundations powerfully inform our approach to the task at hand. They define and motivate our ministry practices.

To be Wesleyan is to be convinced that God is at work in salvific ways in the lives of all people; that love is the most powerful force, and that it is readily available in and through the church by the Holy Spirit; that love is sufficient to transform our congregations into agents of grace, overcome our inhibitions, and dissolve our resistance.

Acknowledgment

Section 2 discusses concrete ways we can understand and value ethnic diversity. We consider how we can:

- Develop cultural awareness
- Understand diverse cultural expressions
- Communicate with cultural sensitivity

Section 2 answers the question: *How do we approach people who are unlike us?*

Chapter 5 gives us the basic principles of cultural awareness—our own cultural situation and the filters through which we interpret different cultural norms. These insights free us from distorted constructs and clear the way for us to build a realistic framework for understanding others.

Chapter 6 outlines the broad cultural categories that characterize people groups. This is the general "where you're coming from" perspective that we need to know in order to connect with people. Exploring cultural models helps us understand how to know ourselves better, and provides us with tools to understand others.

Recognizing that we do not all come from the same cultural framework helps us see differentness as opportunity for bonding rather than a barrier to separate.

Becoming culturally aware positions us to develop culturally sensitive communication skills, the theme of chapter 7. Undoubtedly, miscommunication is a universal challenge; moreso when we try to communicate with those from another cultural context, with a different primary language.

We approach this challenge with the affirmation that communication happens when we put our conversation partner first. This approach is not only practically effective but is also a reflection of God's gracious, costly initiative to communicate with us.

Discernment

Section 3 presents us with case studies of how some pastors are engaging with ethnically diverse families in their communities. This helps us think through what we can learn and apply in our own situations. We conclude with some practical considerations in the process of developing or growing multicultural ministry. Discernment is the final step in multiculturalism:

- Case studies that explore multiculturalism
- Ways to develop cross-cultural relationships
- Practical considerations for developing multicultural ministry

Section 3 answers the question: *What is God doing, and what must we do?*

In chapter 8, we see how God is working in three different churches —different contexts and congregation types, all of which approach multicultural ministry with these common strategies: responding to God's vision by addressing the needs of the community; expressing love by developing long-term, meaningful relationships; and becoming a community that welcomes the stranger.

Chapter 9 considers ways to make community connections, to carry out the vision for serving the community, building friendships, and showing hospitality. In other words, the principles learned from the stories in chapter 8 help us to reflect on what can be done. Reading this chapter will help you and your church engage in the process of discerning what God is doing and how you can participate in his mission in your community. Undoubtedly, this is where the rubber hits the road, and challenges abound. But the rewards are immense—we can witness to the world that the power of the gospel is sufficient to gather "differents" and "unlikes" into one people—the people of God.

In the final chapter, we look at the challenge to reinvent ourselves in terms of mindset, worship styles, and practices based on the insights of previous chapters. We and our congregations are called to become all things to all people, to surrender our own ways in order to fulfill God's vision.

This is the reason we choose to walk through the process of discerning how we need to grow and change in order to become a community of belonging for all kinds of people.

This is a vital, costly, and practical expression of self-giving love.

By the end of our shared journey, with the clarity and conviction of the Holy Spirit, may we rise up and move forward into the great adventure of multicultural ministry.

AWARENESS

▲▼▲

Why Multicultural Ministry?

Who has come to live in our neighborhood?
What is the biblical perspective on ethnic diversity?
How does the Wesleyan tradition inform our ministry approach
in an ethnically diverse context?

These are the questions we consider in this section. At the end, we will find that we have strong sociological, biblical, and theological grounds for engaging in multicultural ministry in ways that honor God and affirm his valuation of the intrinsic worth of all people.

Chapter 1
DEMOGRAPHIC SHIFTS: A MISSIONAL OPPORTUNITY
▼▲▼

The urban centers of the United States and Canada may well be some of the most culturally and linguistically diverse in the world. Urban communities are becoming ethnic clusters, microcosms of the broad spectrum of the nations of the world, a complex diaspora, a richly textured, variegated mosaic of worldviews and ideologies, languages, and cultures. This is all due to sustained and wide-scale migration of the people of the world to North America.

Where you and I now engage in the *missio Dei*, in our small sphere of influence, we have, so to speak, awakened to a new reality—families living in pockets of various ethnicities that have introduced a wealth of different customs, mores, languages, and worldviews—that, for us, is a new world ready to be discovered. Undoubtedly, this cultural landscape presents an exciting moment of opportunity and challenge.

Soong-Chan Rah says in his book *Many Colors,* "God, through his sovereign grace, has brought together many nations, ethnicities, and cultures to the North American continent."[1]

This, now, is the horizon and content of our missional vision and task.

In this chapter, we discover the broad features of the ethnic mosaic that is our present missional opportunity by considering these questions:

- What do we mean by multiculturalism as it concerns the local church mission in a culturally diverse community?
- How is migration impacting our communities?
- What is the general makeup of ethnic clusters?

This is our first step in discovering the rich textures and contours of the community mosaic.

Multiculturalism

In the wide sociological framework of North American culture, multiculturalism is variously understood, based on particular perspectives and contexts. For our purposes, we can think about multiculturalism as appropriate response to cultures other than our own. This response entails a process of awareness, acknowledgment, and discernment.

Awareness

Simply put, multiculturalism is awareness that families from multiple cultures, ethnicities, and languages live in the same geographical space. We recognize that cultural diversity is part of our daily lives. We realize that we share life with all kinds of people, we see ourselves as part of the mosaic, and we embrace a common life in the context of diversity.

Acknowledgment

After we become aware of a shared life, we can choose a deeper level of adjustment. That is, we acknowledge "the rights of ethnic, racial, linguistic, and religious minorities to express their distinct identities and cultures freely."[2] Being multicultural in our outlook means that not only do we think of ourselves as a part of the community mosaic, but we acknowledge that each piece of the mosaic belongs in the community. This perspective frees us to express genuine interest in our neighbors.

Discernment

Acceptance of and interest in our neighbors paves the way for discernment. Thus, multiculturalism finds fullest expression in a commitment to build a network of relationships within a mosaic, to discern, understand, and respect commonalities and distinctions. Simply, everybody is the same; everybody is unique. Discernment is the process of identifying, understanding, and accepting both commonality and differentiation.

To summarize: We understand multiculturalism as intentional, informed, and Christ-filled response to ethnic diversity, and we consider cultural diversity an exciting missional opportunity.

This is a working definition that will guide the discussion in subsequent chapters. So let's briefly reflect on the bearing of our definition on local church ministries in multicultural communities.

Junior Sorzano, pastor of a multicultural congregation in London, Ontario, draws out these ecclesial implications of multiculturalism:

- A local church should reflect the cultural mosaic of the community.
- Awareness, acknowledgment, and discernment must be woven into every aspect of ecclesial life.

In the book *The Integrated Church*, Tracey M. Lewis-Giggetts says, "We'll never truly experience radical, life-giving community if we only hang out with people like us. God didn't choose us based on affinity with us. God turns his enemies and aliens and strangers into his friends and members of his family. True community involves otherness and difference, bringing people together based on values and convictions that go deeper than shared consumer preferences."[3]

As Ken Davis suggests in his article "Multicultural Church Planting Models," we may define a multicultural congregation as "a biblical community of disciples that recognizes, embraces, and affirms a diversity of peoples; is committed to racial reconciliation; and is working out administrative structures that assure the continuation of both unity and diversity."[4]

The North American Mosaic

Urban communities are rapidly changing from monocultural to multicultural due to increased migration to North America from other world areas. Migration has always been a part of the human story. People move. When people move, they and the communities to which they migrate are changed through mutual influence and adaptation. But now, sociologists tell us, we are experiencing accelerated migration.

Unprecedented Global Migration

According to the United Nations World Bank, "In 2015, the number of international migrants worldwide—people residing in a country other than their country of birth—was the highest ever recorded, having reached 244 million (from 232 million in 2013)."[5]

As it concerns the United States and Canada, here's the situation:

In 2015, 46.6 million of the U.S. population and 7.6 million of Canadians were born in another country.[6] This trend is expected to increase. Statisticians expect that by 2065, 46 percent of Americans will be white, 14 percent Asian, and 24 percent Hispanic.[7] In Canada, experts predicted that by 2017, immigrants would account for 22 percent of the population. They predict that by 2036, immigrants will represent between 24.5 and 30.0 percent of the nation's population, compared with 20.7 percent in 2011.

Experts also predict that in 2036, between 55.7 and 57.9 percent of Canada's immigrant population will be Asian-born, up from 44.8 percent they estimated in 2011, while European-born immigrants will drop from 31.6 in 2011 to between 15.4 and 17.8 percent.

Together, immigrants and second-generation individuals could represent nearly one person in two (between 44.2 and 49.7 percent) in 2036, up from 2011 (38.2 percent).[8]

As it concerns the mission of God, these statistics help us become aware, acknowledge, and carefully discern the opportunity set before us. What are the missional implications for the unique communities where we serve? Local churches can only obtain a meaningful and relevant answer as they come to terms with the missional opportunity and begin to pray, reflect, and seek God for vision, passion, and direction for shaping the particular community mosaic he wants to create in and through their congregations.

Reasons for Global Migration

Every year, the United States and Canada welcome immigrants from many world areas who seek educational and professional advancement. Some attend universities to obtain advanced degrees and sometimes remain to build a life and become part of the mosaic. Others come seeking employment. We may broadly categorize these immigrants as seeking opportunities for a better life. However, the greater portion of immigrants in recent years are migrating because life-threatening situations compel them to flee their homelands.[9]

- Refugees
  By the end of 2015, the world was hosting 21.3 million refugees. The number of refugees has increased 55 percent since the end of 2011, largely due to conflict in the Syrian Arab Republic. During 2015 alone, 1.8 million people became refugees, compared to 1.2 million in 2014.

- Conflict & Violence
  About 65.3 million individuals were forcibly displaced by conflict and violence by the end of 2015, 21.3 million of these crossed international

borders. Minors represented nearly 20 percent of first-time asylum applicants in 2015, and more than one-third of forced labor victims worldwide.

• Natural Disasters
More than 19.2 million people were displaced by disasters, primarily weather related, in 110 countries during 2015. The likelihood of being displaced by a disaster today is 60 percent higher than forty years ago.

For these and other reasons, massive migration is a fact of twenty-first-century existence. For the most part, immigrants settle in urban areas throughout the U.S. and Canada.[10] Therefore, the population of our urban centers and their parishes are likely becoming increasingly multiethnic and multilingual.

Mosaic Textures

Awareness, recognition, and discernment (multiculturalism) become a part of our missional approach as we come to terms with these changes, and as we invest in the lives of migrant families—to hear their stories and work with them to make our communities and churches places where they can belong.

The Broad Landscape

Our parishioners are dealing with changes in their daily experiences:
• Cultural diversity influences all dimensions of daily life.
• Rapid cultural adjustments are demanded of social entities, families, and individuals.
• In the shared spaces of common life—the workplace, schools, hospitals, churches, grocery stores—all community members must adjust to change.

This situation offers the church an opportunity to be the cohesive influence that promotes flourishing of the whole community. The fact of cultural diversity must become an important dimension of the way we think about ministry.

The range of ethnicities is another dimension of current migratory patterns.

Within the same zip code, for example, we may find clusters of families from different world areas living side by side. As cultures and worldviews converge, sociological norms are redefined. People dress in a variety of ways, speak various languages, eat different kinds of foods, and engage in multiple social rituals.

The church's challenge is to respect, accept, and transcend differences in order to build meaningful relationships.

Perhaps the most significant implication of mass migration is the intersection of divergent worldviews, philosophies, religious beliefs, and practices that define North Americans' way of being.

This new reality stands in stark contrast to the North American way of life that was previously understood as traditional monoculture. We are challenged to learn afresh how to communicate the gospel and contend for the faith in communities where many deny the Lordship of Jesus Christ.

Building on awareness and acknowledgment (per our definition of multiculturalism), we must acquire discernment. All colors look the same from a distance. All textures also look the same. But as we grow in awareness, and acknowledge diversity as a gift, we develop the ability to discern commonalities and distinctions; that is, we start getting to know our community.

Particularity

We may tend to group all ethnicities together, and assume that these groups share similar customs and values. But in fact, within the complex macrocosm of ethnic diversity, each ethnic group brings its own culture and worldview to its new home. Even within the same ethnic groups, we need to identify and understand subcultures.

Generational Differences

"Given current immigration trends and birth rates, virtually all (93 percent) of the growth of the nation's working-age population between now and 2050 will be accounted for by immigrants and their U.S.-born children, according to a population projection by the Pew Research Center."[11]

As we can see, this is a rapidly growing demographic.

The children of immigrants find themselves living in two worlds, in the tensional space of two identities. Pew Research surveys of Hispanics and Asian Americans—the groups that comprise most of the modern immigration wave—find that roughly six in ten adults in the second generation consider themselves to be a "typical American," about double the share of immigrants who say the same.

Still, most in the second generation also have a strong sense of identity with their ancestral roots. Majorities say they identify themselves most often by their family's country of origin (Mexican, Chinese American) or by a panethnic or racial label (Hispanic or Asian American). Some 37 percent of second-generation Hispanics and 27 percent of second-generation Asian Americans say they most often describe themselves simply as American.[12]

We need to take steps to understand the concerns of this population, their values, the points at which they express their cultural origins, and the points where they prefer to integrate into their environment.

As a preliminary step of rapprochement, we can begin with the awareness of the important differences between immigrant parents and their children, who are often called second generation.

Interracial Families

Another rapidly growing ethnic subculture is the mixed-race population. About one in six (15 percent) married second-generation adults have a spouse of a different race or ethnicity, compared with 8 percent of all immigrants and 8 percent of all U.S. adults. Intermarriage rates are especially high for second-generation Hispanics (26 percent) and Asian Americans (23 percent).[13]

According to a 2015 article in *USA Today*, nearly one in fourteen Americans should be considered multiracial. With interracial marriages and the birth of multiracial babies on the rise, the share of Americans who claim more than one race is expected to grow quickly in coming decades.[14]

The challenges facing multiracial people need to be understood and distinguished from a generic racism agenda. Multiracial families function with at least two sets of cultural mores and norms at home and with a wide range of cultural signals in their daily working environment. They also face challenges of fitting in, of understanding social cues, and of combatting racial prejudice from their own and other cultures.

The church's opportunity is to listen and understand the stories of these individuals and families. And, as we listen and learn each unique story, we embark on the journey of discernment, to develop the sensitivity necessary for meaningful interactions.

Conclusion

In this chapter, we have briefly explored the sociological features of cultural diversity in North America. This overview has given us some insight into the missional challenge and opportunity, and the need for churches to reflect the cultural mosaic of the communities they serve.

Based on this chapter, consider this . . .

- What evidences of diversity do you see in your community?

- Look around at the grocery store, school, doctors' offices—who lives in your neighborhood?

- Where can you go to find out where people have come from, the challenges they face, and other details about them?

- How can your local church connect with immigrant clusters in your community?

Chapter 2
DIVERSITY IN GOD'S GOOD CREATION

▼▲▼

In the previous chapter, we discussed the increasing cultural diversity of North American communities. The fact that this phenomenon has drawn us into a dialogue indicates that we recognize some of the missional implications and opportunities. The first chapter hinted at avenues for connectedness that the church might adopt, as we defined multiculturalism in terms of awareness, acknowledgment, and discernment. But before we advance, full steam ahead, to get to know our neighbors, we need to examine how Scripture informs our multicultural mission. Joe Knight unfolds the beginnings of the human story to convincingly argue that diversity is in the DNA of God's good creation.

On Being Human

Joe Knight believes the local church should seek to reflect the ethnic makeup of the community it serves because, by nature, the church is a place where people from any socioeconomic context can belong. This idea is inherent in the biblical narrative, rooted in and derived from the grand sweep of revelation as it unfolds through a succession of pivotal events in the full story of God's covenant history with his creation.

To validate this premise, we must begin at the beginning: We must identify the biblical view of what it means to be human, in the collectivities of nations, cities, and communities. Once we start considering who we are from a biblical perspective, our worldview and self-understanding begin to shift. We identify and renounce false premises that have become embedded in our minds and that drive our reactions and choices.

Consider, for example, these questions:

• *Similarity*

How similar are we? Considering the obvious differences between the vast spectrum of cultures and continents, is there a floor of commonality—human universals experienced by everyone—that could form the basis for meaningful cross-cultural comprehension and authentic community? Do all people in all parts of the world grapple with the same fundamental issues?

• *Equality*

Are we one master race within the human family?

Does Scripture establish racial equality or does it elevate one race as the model for the other races to emulate? Of foremost importance is the matter of equality. Mutual acceptance between individuals across ethnic lines is presumed possible only if an equivalence view prevails.

• *Peace*

Could we see a dove in the place of a bomb? Is there a solution with enough strength that can remedy deeply rooted ethnic hostility, especially those in which the memories of atrocity or betrayal remain fresh?

• *Insight*

Are there keys of understanding that can encourage harmony within the multicultural church? In the face of interethnic misunderstanding or controversy, is there a theologically shaped vocabulary of race that truly enlightens, promotes honest dialogue, adjusts faulty thinking, increases mutual empathy, fosters goodwill, and hastens resolution? If so, where can that discussion happen?

• *Grouping*

What's the balance between ethnic clustering and transethnic belonging? In a local church, when should we consider separate subgrouping with one's "own kind" valid and healthy and when does it limit the greater good of Christ's body or reinforce group-think? Some people of all ethnic heritages seem culture-locked, forming parallel societies without any genuine interaction with those outside of their own tight-knit communities. Is that a problem?

• *Belonging*

How can we achieve dynamic synergy and participatory belonging by tapping into the rich reservoir of diversity? What can a church do to integrate people from multiple cultures into a community where personal belonging is experienced in an intentional process of acceptance, sincerity, frankness, laughter, trust, sharing Jesus, and prayer—and where newer ethnic members become active contributors to the larger mosaic?

The biblical view of humanness points us in the right direction for answering these questions.

• *Ethnic Identity*

Does Scripture portray human beings and their ethnic identities in a manner that prepares the way for cultural diversity in local churches? How does God view diversity?

In looking to Scripture for answers, if we find grounds for the undoubted value of all people to God, then we have not only biblical grounds for ethnically diverse congregations, but also a biblical mandate.

Creational Diversity

Creational diversity is neither a problem to be solved nor an ideal to be deified, but a gift to be gratefully celebrated in the unified worship of God.[1] The good creation, the product of Trinitarian action, is diverse and positive in all its diversity. The beauty and harmony of the good creation is shalom, the epitome of widespread wholeness and health.[2]

Shalom is the experience, on the human side, of the divine goodness and joy that find expression in the complex harmony of the good creation. Thus, Genesis 1 presents a hymn of creation to the praise of a Creator whose attributes of goodness and power were made manifest through all of his handiwork.

Diversity is the product of God's creative action; diversity is the nature of the creation over which God continues to rule with sovereign, providential care.

Intrinsic Human Value

Next is the intrinsic value conferred through the *imago Dei* upon every human being.[3] People individually and collectively share a transcendent relationship that is unique and enduring. On the sixth creative day God said, "Let Us make man in Our image, according to Our likeness; . . . God created man in His own image, in the image of God He created him; male and female He created them" (Gen. 1:26–27, NASB).

Adam was given his name from the ground from which he came (Gen. 2:7).[4] In the absence of a human father he stands outside of ethnicity. Presented in the biblical narrative as the first man, he represents a new classification within creation. He was "a single human being . . . humankind, mankind, a class of being created by God without regard to sex, with a focus as a class of creature, distinct from animals, plants, or even spiritual beings" (Gen. 1:26).[5]

This biblical portrayal affirms the value and honor the Creator confers on all people, and provides the basis for human rights.[6] The image of God is upon all human beings, conferring value regardless of any other designation.

Notice that Seth, born outside the gates of Eden, nevertheless retains the "likeness of God" (Gen. 5:1–2, NASB) while shaped by the fallen condition of his father (Gen. 5:3). The *imago Dei,* however marred and disfigured, issues in explicit divine protections of the human species so that the unlawful removal of human life from earth is explicitly forbidden (Gen. 9:6).

The Genesis account of the creation of humankind provides us with an unassailable rationale for intentionally developing congregational life that reflects the value the Creator places on his image bearers. It sets the agenda for ecclesial action that seeks to draw all into a community of acceptance; where people from every nation, tribe, and language can come to know him to whom we all belong, and to experience in redemptive fellowship the power of the cross to bring each one to restoration of the *imago Dei* in Christ.

Ethnic Subgroups

Ethnic subgroups reflect the rich diversity of the creation and its Creator.

Adam's race contains many family units, which further subdivide into clans and tribes. Genesis 9 and 10 provide crucial insights into the biblical view of ethnicity that inform our understanding of multicultural ministry.

The rise of nations, cultures, tribes, and clans suggests that God's ideal is diversity. After the earth was destroyed through the flood, humanity experienced a new beginning as Noah's three sons received the same command that had been issued to Adam and Eve, to be fruitful and multiply and fill the earth (Gen. 9:1; 1:28).[7]

The Table of Nations in Genesis 10 reflects compliance by these brothers, tracing their respective genealogies without a hint of censure.

The placement of the Table of Nations in the narrative reinforces this positive appraisal. The text introduces the family of nations with distinct languages and cultures in Genesis 10:5, 20, and 31, that is, before God's judgment against the Tower of Babel project. The significance of this insight is that each subgroup received unqualified legitimacy. Ethnic designations indelibly identify each person's particular place of belonging within the larger human family in the present life[8] and, as we shall see, this will be carried on into the next life as well.

Ethnic Equality

Within that vast ethnic constellation, we find equality and differentiation.

The Table validates every ethnic family and tribal unit within the whole.[9] Some may argue that Abraham and his progeny were chosen and set apart from all other nations in the covenant God made with him, so that Israel may seem to have been granted an advantage or preference over all others. But this assumption must be immediately set aside since it is clear that God chose Abraham not to be above other nations, but to be his instrument to bless all nations (Gen. 22:18).

Even as revelation light comes to full fruition in incarnation, crucifixion, resurrection, and Pentecost, in the proclamation of the glorious gospel of Jesus Christ, the apostles are called to adjust to God's valuation of all (Gal. 3:28; Acts 15:9; Eph. 2:14).

As the Apostle Paul declares to the Athenians: "From one ancestor he made all nations to inhabit the whole earth, and he allotted the times of their existence and the boundaries of the places where they would live, so that they would search for God and perhaps grope for him and find him" (Acts 17:26–27, NRSV).

Distributive Providence

Tribal groupings and families reflect the providential care of a loving Creator on behalf of all individuals: "Father of orphans and protector of widows is God in his holy habitation. God gives the desolate a home to live in" (Ps. 68:5–6, NRSV).[10]

Family units are built into the fabric of all societies from the dawn of creation (Gen. 2:24–25; Heb. 13:4). Adam's race, sectioned into smaller units like an ever-spreading honeycomb, permits rapid population growth without threatening individual protections.

The Sum Greater than Its Parts

Family clusters to which individuals belong are not set in tension with humanity as a whole. While each ethnic subgroup receives unquestionable validation and permanence, it, nevertheless, receives only secondary impor-

tance as one part of greater humanity. The Table of Nations presents a unified world of seventy nations, "a numerical symbol of fullness and wholeness.
God's blessing covers the whole earth."[11]

This Table, unique in the ancient world,[12] conveys two theological messages:

It points to "one world governed by one God,"[13] summarized in Genesis
11:1 as "all the earth."

It represents "the *ecumene*, that is, a group of peoples that are so inter-
locked by give-and-take that they constitute one world civilization . . . Inter-
nationalism precedes nationalism and provincialism."[14]

The ever-expanding range of subgroups within it detracts nothing from
this solidarity, which provides the human family with a basis of respect, reciprocity, and delight across all subgroups. It affirms that "all of humanity, despite geographical and linguistic differences, shares a common origin. In this
is humankind's nobility and inherent value."[15] The *imago Dei*, without eras-
ing lesser semblances and provincial loyalties, simply overrides them. Salvation will celebrate this intercontinental assembly as part of divine creation.

Conclusion

A positive view of ethnicity reflects God's rich diversity as shown in the
opening pages of Scripture.

Diversity is a fundamental dimension of God's original plan, his creative
differentiation without stratification, providential care distributed throughout human existence and subservient to the greater whole of humanity that
shares the greatest likeness in the *imago Dei*.

Yet, we need to come to terms with the reality of fractured human relationships, universal human alienation. Our brief exploration of the beginnings of human civilization immediately shows us that this fracture is not
God's design. Yet, it is so definitive of human relationality in a fallen world
that we have come to accept fracture as a sociological normality that we must
work with rather than repair.

We have imposed the distortion of human relationality upon human diversity so that the concepts of differentness and being fractured have been
conflated into a single entity. In other words, we tend to think of diversity as
the cause of being fractured, rather than being fractured as a result of fallen-
ness an anomaly in God's good creation, a distortion of God's vision of hu-

manness, a threat to shalom. Redemption speaks the truth about this human calamity, speaks against acceptance of the apparent synonymity of fracture and differentness, speaks for celebration of differentness and healing of our wound. The nature of redemption in Christ and how it speaks to this brokenness is our topic in the next chapter.

Based on this chapter, consider this . . .

- Reconciliation: The Bible's positive instruction on racial identity provides resources for reconciliation. How might reconciliation become a characteristic of a local church?

- Human Rights: Misinformed teaching breeds malformed practice. Deficient racial views injure entire groups of people, all God's image-bearers. Distorted anthropologies lie hidden behind every imaginable social ostracism, imperialistic coercion, dehumanizing stereotype, and genocidal atrocity. Consider the transformative power of God's truth: How can we include biblical anthropology in the curriculum of the local church?

- Fulfill the Great Commission: Building the larger scaffolding of human creation before sharing the Jesus story with our foreign neighbors provides the gospel with a universal structure on which to anchor itself. In the New Testament, God did not take a sudden interest in the nations. They were on his heart from the very beginning of time and of Scripture. Are we willing to introduce this dimension of the gospel into the life of the church?

- Diversity & the Knowledge of God: Multiple cultural perspectives provide a fuller view of the God we worship. This God is not white, not black, not red, not brown. We serve a God who transcends locality and cannot be reduced by any single culture. How can the Christian community more vividly portray God's valuation of diversity?

Chapter 3

NEW CREATION AND DIVERSITY

▼▲▼

The previous chapter helped us recognize that diversity is embedded in the DNA of God's good creation—not as an anomaly but as God's norm for shalom. God speaks an organized differentiation into existence. In this grand theater of his glory, he introduces humankind, the capstone, *chef d'oeuvre* of his creation. Diversity is part of God's vision for human society.

The fall introduced a fracture in human relationships, including the erroneous identification of diversity as the cause of fractured relationships. As a result, we wall ourselves into monocultural enclaves as a perceived way to protect ourselves from the unknown and the different.

The New Testament points us to God's way to take down the walls and find a new creation, to restore the joyous mosaic that is intrinsic to the divine mosaic of shalom.

This chapter explores the new creation in Christ and its redemptive power to rescue human society from brokenness to wholeness—to the creation of something new, a restoration of the very DNA of human relationality.

The DNA of the New Creation

The story of the church's beginnings demonstrates that cultural diversity is presupposed as an important dimension of what it means to be the people of God. The church is God's new creation in Christ by the Holy Spirit. The New Testament gives us insight as to the character of the new creation, the community of the faithful.

Divine Initiative

As told in Acts 2, the Day of Pentecost marked the birth of the church and the beginning of the new creation. This event was characterized by cultural diversity:

> When the day of Pentecost arrived, they were all together in one place. And suddenly there came from heaven a sound like a mighty rushing wind, and it filled the entire house where they were sitting. And divided tongues as of fire appeared to them and rested on each one of them. And they were all filled with the Holy Spirit and began to speak in other tongues as the Spirit gave them utterance.
>
> Now there were dwelling in Jerusalem Jews, devout men from every nation under heaven. And at this sound the multitude came together, and they were bewildered, because each one was hearing them speak in his own language. And they were amazed and astonished, saying, "Are not all these who are speaking Galileans? And how is it that we hear, each of us in his own native language?
>
> Parthians and Medes and Elamites and residents of Mesopotamia, Judea and Cappadocia, Pontus and Asia, Phrygia and Pamphylia, Egypt and the parts of Libya belonging to Cyrene, and visitors from Rome, both Jews and proselytes, Cretans and Arabians—*we hear them telling in our own tongues the mighty works of God.* (Acts 2:1–11, ESV, emphasis mine)

The baptism of the Holy Spirit led to Jesus Christ being proclaimed as risen Lord to people from across the Roman Empire. This audience heard the gospel in their own languages.

What does this tell us about God's approach to cultural diversity regarding the proclamation of the Good News? He intends that all nations should come to know Christ and participate in the new creation.

The linguistic miracle that allowed people to hear and understand the message reminds us that God's gracious initiative is the cause of the new creation. God is ready to empower the church to take the initiative and be sufficiently flexible to draw in people from every nation and language.

We may also infer that local churches, the church in microcosm throughout all nations and ages, should reflect God's vision for the community of faith's composition: a community that mirrors divine initiative by extending grace and mercy to people across the grand sweep of human diversity and welcoming them into a community of disciples where they can belong.

Overcoming Predispositions

In the story of the early church, things went along nicely: the apostles preached the gospel and aside from persecutions happening here and there, everybody was doing great. Then God intervened again. He had a conversation with Peter:

> The next day, as they were on their journey and approaching the city, Peter went up on the housetop about the sixth hour to pray. And he became hungry and wanted something to eat, but while they were preparing it, he fell into a trance and saw the heavens opened and something like a great sheet descending, being let down by its four corners upon the earth.
>
> In it were all kinds of animals and reptiles and birds of the air. And there came a voice to him: "Rise, Peter; kill and eat."
>
> But Peter said, "By no means, Lord; for I have never eaten anything that is common or unclean."
>
> And the voice came to him again a second time, "What God has made clean, do not call common." This happened three times, and the thing was taken up at once to heaven. (Acts 10:9-16, ESV)

This vision prepared Peter for a shift in his mindset that would allow him to declare the gospel to Gentiles. Thus far, the gospel had primarily reached Jews. God wanted Peter to comprehend the message—the gospel was for everybody, and Peter had to get on board with God's vision. "Peter replied, 'I see very clearly that God shows no favoritism. In every nation he accepts those who fear him and do what is right'" (Acts 10:34–35, NLT).

We may draw important insights from this event:

- God once again takes the initiative and calls on his servant to take the initiative to embrace Gentiles, in this case Cornelius.
- God recognizes the difficulties associated with asking Peter to overcome his cultural predisposition.
- The graphic display of the clean/unclean contrast powerfully demonstrated that God meant business.
- Peter needed a powerful, defining moment of realization in order to set aside deep-rooted religious custom.

This vision shows the emphasis God placed on his disciples accepting Gentiles. God's intention is to create a community of acceptance that requires our overcoming cultural dispositions—a countercultural community that would demonstrate what new creation looks like.

These features of the church's early days suggest that we might need to examine our personal and congregational predispositions and ask God to show us how we may take the initiative in connecting with neighbors from different lands.

God's Wide Horizon

Paul wrote to the Ephesians:

So then, remember that at one time you were Gentiles in the flesh—called "the uncircumcised" by those called "the circumcised," which is done in the flesh by human hands. At that time you were without Christ, excluded from the citizenship of Israel, and foreigners to the covenants of promise, without hope and without God in the world. But now in Christ Jesus, you who were far away have been brought near by the blood of Christ. For he is our peace, who made both groups one and tore down the dividing wall of hostility. (Eph. 2:11–14, CSB)

In explaining their new status in Christ, Paul told the Ephesian Christians that they were no longer on the outside of God's new creation. They had been brought inside; they belonged. The wall of hostility and separation that kept them out was dissolved in Christ.

The harmony of cultures is inherent in the gospel itself. As it concerns our missional objectives, the important realization is that pursuing cultural diversity, overcoming cultural barriers, and developing culturally diverse congregations is not meant, biblically speaking, to be a missional strategy simply so that we can plant more churches or be more successful.

Instead, the gospel message assumes the value of diversity, transcends cultural barriers, and proclaims to all the new creation in which there is neither Jew nor Greek, male nor female, bond nor free (Gal. 3:28).

Culture and Counterculture

In Acts 15, the young church had to deal with an important question: Should Gentile believers be bound by the socioreligious customs of the dominant (Jewish) culture?

Some men came down from Judea and began to teach the brothers: "Unless you are circumcised according to the custom prescribed by Moses, you cannot be saved." After Paul and Barnabas had engaged them in serious argument and debate, Paul and Barnabas and some others were appointed to go up to the apostles and elders in Jerusalem about this issue. . . .

When they arrived at Jerusalem, they were welcomed by the church, the apostles, and the elders, and they reported all that God had done with them. But some of the believers who belonged to the party of the Pharisees stood up and said, "It is necessary to circumcise them and to command them to keep the law of Moses."

The apostles and the elders gathered to consider this matter. After there had been much debate, Peter stood up and said to them: "Brothers and sisters, you are aware that in the early days God made a choice among you, that by my mouth the Gentiles would hear the gospel message and believe. And God, who knows the heart, bore witness to them by giving them the Holy Spirit, just as he also did to us. He made no distinction between us and them, cleansing their hearts by faith. Now then, why are you testing God by putting a yoke on the disciples' necks that neither our ancestors nor we have been able to bear? On the contrary, we believe that we are saved through the grace of the Lord Jesus in the same way they are. . . ."

After they stopped speaking, James responded: "Brothers and sisters, listen to me. Simeon has reported how God first intervened to take from the Gentiles a people for his name. . . . Therefore, in my judgment, we should not cause difficulties for those among the Gentiles who turn to God, but instead we should write to them to abstain from things polluted by idols, from sexual immorality, from eating anything that has been strangled, and from blood" (Acts 15:1–2, 4–11, 13–14, 19, CSB).

We may infer that in the ecclesial situation of diverse cultural and religious customs, the guideline for all is not "what we've always done," but what seems right to us all and to the Holy Spirit (Acts 15:28).

Further, in the ecclesial situation with a dominant culture, the dominant culture should be accommodating of the newer, smaller culture to the extent afforded by the gospel of grace. Such an approach reflects beautifully the gracious divine initiative.

And finally, in the situation of cultural diversity, the community of faith can only move forward by Spirit-filled, open communication. Differences must be worked through rather than worked around, acknowledged and respected rather than ignored. Willingness to change must characterize our approach to such conversations.

Opposition

Another feature of cultural diversity in the early church was opposition to diversity. The issue brought to light and apparently resolved in Acts 15 kept cropping up. In Paul's letter to the Galatians, he chastised them for preaching a gospel of Jesus *and* circumcision. He earned critics and enemies because of his stance.

But Paul was not merely taking the side of the Gentiles. His insistence on this point had to do with the gospel itself—a message of Christ *and* _____ was no gospel.

For Paul, proclaiming Good News entailed proclamation to the Gentiles, because a fundamental element of the Good News was to include all people. He took a stand because the very nature of the gospel he preached demanded that no social, political, cultural, or economic boundaries should bar the proclamation of the gospel and the inclusion of people into the community of faith.

We should not be surprised that when we move from "what we've always done" to God's vision of new creation, we find ourselves in conflict with hidden agendas and predispositions that favor a dominant culture and are less in harmony with the gospel.

We are called to proclaim Christ and to take a stand in harmony with this proclamation. We are called to do so with grace, patience, and prayer, always bearing in mind how challenging it is to surrender our constructs. But the message of the cross calls us to surrender our constructs and be transformed by the renewing of our minds. And we must be faithful to this promise and command.

Missional and Ecclesial Touchstones

Twenty-first century North American faith communities are descendants of the New Testament church. Jesus is rightly served when we derive our rationale and working philosophy from these biblical roots. He is rightly served when we strive to faithfully allow biblical principles to drive our ministry strategies. We are doing the right thing by embracing cultural diversity in our faith communities.

Here are some of principles we can extract from the New Testament context to inform our ecclesiology. As we apply these principles in context, the result will be a unique mosaic characterized by God's vision. We are called to approach cultural diversity by developing awareness of our context, acknowledging God's valuation of individuals, and discerning practical ways to make our local church an extension of the biblical narrative. These principles would identify such a local church:

Diversity Is Gospel

The New Testament tells us that diversity is not something we have to embrace as a missional strategy. It is in the DNA of the new creation. The gospel calls us to understand the community of faith as a place of belonging for all individuals, to work toward transcending the anomalies of those who are fractured by systematically operating on the basis of God's valuation of all people.

Diversity Is Countercultural

Cultural clusters exist because we are more comfortable in cultural clusters. We prefer monoculture, monolingual communities and churches. And when attempt harmony of cultures, we encounter the challenge of a dominant culture that seeks to assert itself. Yet, to be faithful to the gospel, we have to deliberately develop strategies to overcome these tendencies and replace them with an ecclesial habitus that harmonizes with the gospel message.

Diversity Is the Space of Belonging

Diverse congregations declare a powerful message to the world through their very existence—that the gospel is for all people, that all people can know Christ and enjoy shalom in his name. The reverse is also true, as we may assert by answering the question: What is the message proclaimed by a monocultural congregation in an ethnically diverse neighborhood? The challenge is to decisively draw on available resources in order for local churches to reflect the community mosaic. And this we will do by the help of God.

Conclusion

Cultural diversity is a present reality. Based on the biblical witness, we cannot ignore this reality, nor can we build fences to keep ourselves in and others out. Diversity is an important dimension of what it means to be God's redeemed people, the new creation. This means that we can be optimistic, that the church must take the initiative to introduce diversity as part of ecclesial culture, and that we can be bold in this approach because we are simply being obedient to the *missio Dei.*

Optimism

Jesus Christ is building his church by the power of the Holy Spirit. We have certain hope that he enables what he requires. Thus, diversity is not something we have to make happen, but something that God is doing—and we are required to get on board with his agenda.

Initiative

God takes the initiative toward us. Every time. This is grace. He reveals himself. He comes to us. He speaks. His new creation, the church, is called to take the initiative of grace; we build a bridge not for those on the other side to cross over to us, but for us to get to the other side.

Boldness

As the new creation—the church—we can boldly set aside our predispositions and consider others, not in our learned sociocultural frame, but to regard each person as loved by God: "For the love of Christ controls us, because we have concluded this: that one has died for all, therefore all have died; and he died for all, that those who live might no longer live for themselves but for him who for their sake died and was raised. From now on, therefore, we regard no one according to the flesh" (2 Cor. 5:14–16, ESV).

Based on this chapter, consider this . . .

Maybe now we can look at our congregations with new eyes, uncover the true basis of our fellowship, the real common ground, and begin to be explicit about these things.

- How intentional are we in embracing minority groups?

- What are some challenges we face in reflecting God's vision for his new creation?

Maybe, we can now look at our neighbors with different lenses, with the confidence that, differentiation aside, we are all connected and we have ways to build relationships.

- What can we do to show our neighbors that we accept them?

- How would people from other cultures feel in our fellowship?

- How would we react when cultures collide?

Chapter 4

WESLEYAN PERSPECTIVES FOR MULTICULTURAL ENGAGEMENT

▼▲▼

Biblical and sociological perspectives indicate the sociological landscape and the missional approach evoked by cultural diversity. Reader, you would be justified in also asking, "What about our Wesleyan roots?"

This chapter identifies principles for multicultural ministry that arise from our Wesleyan foundations. Wesleyanism introduces optimistic insights for the task under consideration.

The reality of prevenient grace means we can surely expect God to clear the way for meaningful transcultural connections.

The holiness message affirms that believers can love with the holy love of God.

It follows that differentness is no longer an insurmountable barrier; instead, the capacity to love those who are different from us powerfully demonstrates God's transformative power in and through his people.

As the people of God, we become the means of grace through whom the life-giving Spirit heals, restores, and transforms people who are different into a redeemed and redemptive mosaic.

Prevenient Grace

Prevenient grace incites us to optimism, because, at bottom, it means that the Holy Spirit is now and always at work in ways that lead to salvation.

Wesleyan optimism is grounded in the assuredness of universal atonement, the grace of our Lord Jesus Christ at work in the world by the Holy Spirit:

John Wesley had a broad sense that all human beings, societies, cultures, and religious systems were within the scope of God's gaze—embracing neighbors, strangers, friends, and enemies. Likewise, God is already at work within those cultures and many of the religious systems by natural revelation or prevenient grace—that action of God, the Holy Spirit, whereby human beings are given clues, foretastes, of God's abiding presence in the world, drawing them toward reconciliation.[1]

Even before we encounter someone, grace has been working in that person's life. We may expect that lines of connection are already drawn and established. As we seek new relationships, we pray for discernment of how the Holy Spirit has prepared us and others for redemptive relationship. We reflect on how we can operate in harmony with what God is doing. We ask, "How might God use me and my faith community in his redemptive action?"

God Moving Ahead

This preparatory work of the Spirit is a solid basis to see past what might be stop signs and press forward to discern what the Spirit is doing. Stop signs become visible when we try to get close to people. We might be able to exchange courtesies and pleasantries with our neighbors without getting into conversations and situations that reveal conflicting worldviews. But what can we do when we encounter deep differences—especially regarding the God we worship and, consequently, our valuation of individuals?

I remember the progression in one of my own close relationships with someone of another culture and faith. At first the relationship had little challenge. I showed love by small acts of kindness, and I was open about my faith and ministry. My friend appreciated my willingness to spend time with her, even though she was not a Christian. Our friendship had moved to such a place of comfort that we could be quiet together without any tension.

And so, out of the silence, my friend burst out with a shocking remark, "All the problems in the world are because of those people!"

When I asked, "Which people?" she told me how a certain race had corrupted the entire universe. This blew me away! This could not be my lovely friend holding this viewpoint! That was a stop sign.

I had to make a choice. I could shift the conversation to something inconsequential and pretend she had said nothing that offended me as a Christian; I could respond with an aggressive negation of everything she had said; or I could do something else. I couldn't figure out what that something else could be.

I did not engage that day, because I wasn't sure if I could handle the situation properly. But after a few days of reflection and prayer, I waited for an opportunity. And, without referring to that conversation, I introduced my own views "You know, I think everybody, all kinds of people, make the world better or worse, depending on our relationship with God." And so, I shared about God, fallen humankind, and salvation.

This is what I mean about pushing past stop signs. In fact, I think that stop signs are not really stop signs; they are indicators of the Spirit's nudging, challenging constructs, preparing a person to hear the truth.

The reason we dare to press is because we are convinced that the Holy Spirit is at work, breaking barriers, shaking false constructs, and preparing the way for the truth of Jesus Christ.

Thus, as Dan Sheffield suggests, "A Wesleyan response to the stranger of a different religious or cultural system is that of dialogue and discernment, seeking to understand where God has already been drawing, awakening, justifying and sanctifying."[2]

The fact that God is at work means that we must be attentive and develop skills of discernment in order to notice signs of need, spiritual hunger, and readiness. This can only take place in relationships.

Prevenient grace compels a response from us—to invest in getting to know people; to share life through meals, conversations, troubles; to pray. We pray for direction and discernment, for making connections with those who are part of the ripe harvest, for receptivity, and for effectiveness.

Visibility

We discern what God is doing by developing relationships. But how can relationships happen? It is so easy for us to live in our own communities. Since we are pastors, most of the people we know and spend time with are believers. The church is our world. We can spend all our time in our own world and become really closed off from what is happening around us. It is important to find ways to be visible to the community.

This is my present challenge. For many years, I was bivocational—one foot in the church, the other in a public university. I had many relationships with people of other religions. Now, as a full-time pastor, I can easily spend all my time doing church. I have to be proactive and brave to get myself into places where I can get to know people who are unlike me. I imagine it might be the same for many pastors. We have to become visible in order to discern where the Holy Spirit is at work outside the church.

Prevenient grace as a present reality challenges us to step outside the faith community and participate in the broader community. We do not need to construct barriers to protect us from being contaminated by sin. Grace is greater than sin. Taking grace into sin will assuredly destroy sin. This is how we go where God is at work, and we change the world:

> Christian communities operating within a Wesleyan orientation will participate in public conversation about cultural difference. Wesley and the Methodists contributed to many conversations in the public sphere throughout the 18th century and beyond. Wesley was concerned for "a reformation of manners" throughout English society. He referred to many public behaviors and civil practices that he believed did not conform to a biblical worldview, including imprisoning debtors, oppressive child labor, prison conditions, and slavery. Wesley was educated, well-read, and articulate to speak or write on many of the current affairs of his day, which he did.[3]

Praying for direction, for opportunity, for wisdom to use our voice effectively, for grace to be a redemptive influence accompanies our involvement in the life of the parish.

Cooperating with God

How might God use our faith community? We want to be welcoming. But the decisive point is willingness to be welcoming in ways that may be costly, at the expense of our own comfort and convenience. Genuinely welcoming the stranger is cooperation with the Holy Spirit. It arises from the conviction that the very fact that people have come to our church signals the prevenient work of the Holy Spirit.

When we receive visitors as being God-sent, we embrace them as long-lost relatives. We are full of joy and ready to make any necessary accommodation so they feel at home.

A Wesleyan orientation to a culturally diverse community would suggest that Christians from other cultural frameworks are invited, offered hospitality, and welcomed into the Wesleyan congregation where they desire to fellowship. This, in fact, becomes a missional, contextual, response to a culturally diverse neighborhood. Rather than "ghetto-izing" believers of other cultures, all are welcome in the Wesleyan congregation—a powerful symbol of the transformative power of the Christian gospel that breaks down walls.[4]

Genuine welcome gives everyone a voice, a place to belong and serve. Our challenge and opportunity is to honestly consider those aspects of congregational life that may not send a welcoming message.

However much we may like the way we've always done things, or however well we do things, genuine welcome means we have to change to adjust to others. Honest conversations such as, "How can we create a sense of belonging?" are part of the life of a community that affirms prevenient grace.

The dominant culture of a congregation that is ready for costly alignment with prevenient grace will make the adjustments that will send a message of welcome to the community: "We welcome those who are different from ourselves. Will we now allow their voices and their contributions to shape our processes and practices? Christian communities operating within a Wesleyan orientation will include the voices and insights of their brothers and sisters in Christ from other cultural backgrounds into the processes and practices of their congregation."[5]

Love the Stranger

Love is a choice to know and be known through costly self-giving.

Unconditional love reaches out to the other, courageously choosing vulnerability, rejection, and betrayal. Human power is insufficient to generate love between individuals.

The Wesleyan tradition affirms that God's love can so fill the heart and restore our capacity for genuine relationality that we are empowered to engage in the great risk of loving.

For Wesley, "Universal love [is] not confined to one sect or party, not restrained to those who agree with him in opinions, or in outward modes of worship, or to those who are allied to [us] by blood or recommended by nearness of place. Neither [do we] love those only that love [us], or that are endeared to [us] by intimacy of acquaintance . . . It soars above all these scanty bounds, embracing neighbors and strangers, friends, and enemies."[6]

Allowing God to gather a community of people who are different from each other in our place of ministry means taking love seriously.

Love, as we Wesleyans understand it—love, as the essence of the people of God, the compelling motivation for who we are and how we live—necessarily commits us to preferring or favoring others above ourselves.

Understanding

We demonstrate love by seeking to understand where the other person is coming from. Thus, we learn to listen, to take the time to build enough trust so that people tell us their stories. And when we hear those stories we understand the other's worldview. In fact, when the Bible says we must love our enemies, it means we try to understand why our enemy is our enemy—the griefs, betrayals, and brokenness that have led to the fracture of relationships.

Love means we seek to understand the world from another person's perspective.

Acceptance

Without realizing it, we sometimes think that loving someone means we need to change the way that person sees the world. It is a big jump, only possible by the grace of God, to accept the perspective or worldview of the other—perhaps starkly different from ours, perhaps so deeply anti-gospel that we want nothing to do with it. Acceptance is not agreement. Acceptance ascribes value to someone, a stance that says, "You are more than what you believe; you are known and loved by God; I want to know you and love you."

Acceptance is a requirement for a relationship that is authentically human. Surprisingly, we are not called to change people. We are, however, called to influence people, or rather, to allow the Holy Spirit to influence people through us. But in order for others to be receptive to our influence, we need to accept them.

Availability

Love finds its highest expression when we understand and accept individuals with sharply hostile worldviews, and we are readily available to serve them, receive them into our homes, and extend the hand of fellowship. This is the hard work and the sacrificial riskiness of loving. We face hostility and accept that we are called to make this journey with the other in Christ's name.

We Wesleyans embrace a theology of power and optimism. We are witnesses that God's love transforms, heals, and redeems us and others through us. But we also know that life lived in self-giving and self-forgetfulness is painful and is an overt face-to-face engagement with forces of destruction and hate. We live within the range of enemy fire, so to speak. We have planted our feet on enemy territory. The enemy of beauty, love, harmony, and shalom will not give ground without a fight. So we must be prepared for slow progress, for resistance, for setbacks.

But there is no other way forward, except through the walls of resistance. The very fact that we are ready to walk through these walls witnesses to the power of holy love. This kind of offensive action can only be carried out by the community of the faithful working together. And we must at all times pray.

Means of Grace

The community of the faithful is the means through which the Holy Spirit works to draw all kinds of people to faith. We have the opportunity to be a redemptive influence precisely at the point where cultures converge and displacement has made people vulnerable, lonely, isolated, and confused. Immigrants deal with challenges of adjustment over many years. Working, going to school, to the doctor, to the grocery store—everything about day-to-day living requires learning new ways. Right here is the opportunity for the local church. We can give help, hope, stability, and fellowship. We can be the source of encouragement and strength.

Dan Sheffield says, "It is precisely . . . [the] interface between the wider multicultural, pluralistic society . . . and the challenge of authentic engagement with one's different neighbor that causes alienation in our society. It is here that I believe Wesleyan theology and practice can lead to loving, reconciling, healing, including, grace-enabling relationships across the barriers, without which intercultural citizenship is just an exercise in good intentions."[7]

As Sheffield remarks, the differences of immigrants introduce a sense of alienation in society. Dissimilarities make people suspicious.

The church, grounded in the Wesleyan conviction that Christ's love overcomes barriers, has the opportunity to be in the vanguard for moving people groups from isolated coexistence to a community that shares life.

What does it mean for a congregation to be means of grace to its community?

First, let's think about how means of grace function in the church. The people of God partake of means of grace—primarily, the sacraments, prayer, and preaching. We believe that the combination of these habits results in a habitus through which the Holy Spirit draws us into deeper fellowship with God and one another, continually transforming us into the image of Christ.

Now, think about how we can together become the habitus through which the Holy Spirit draws others into the same fellowship. To be the means of grace means that we are the body of Christ—the avenue through which God incarnates his love. Love becomes concrete through our demeanor, disposition, words, and actions. Love becomes concrete in the culture of the congregation, that indescribable "we," the ethos, the "what people are saying about us."

We are means of grace to the world to the extent that love shapes ecclesial culture.

Realizing that God is at work in our midst, shaping us by love into the means of grace for others, is a mighty source of renewal for a congregation and a catalyst for change. We carefully consider the imperfections we may carry in our common life as a church that may obscure love and impede our function as means of grace. Mindsets, interests, agendas, and personal preferences may run counter to the moving of the Holy Spirit.

Perhaps, a good place for us to start is to ask ourselves how we and our congregations can allow the Spirit to align us to be an effective means of grace. Once we start moving closer to who God wants us to be, we can consider how to proactively and purposefully develop strategies to become the place that influences the community with a sense of cohesiveness.

Does being the means of grace mean we have to be multicultural? Great question. I don't know for sure. There are many healthy, effective monocultural congregations. But I don't think we can afford to choose to be monocultural because being multicultural is too hard. We need to let the Holy Spirit rule the church.

Sheffield advocates multicultural congregations as a Wesleyan expression of God's mission:

A Wesleyan orientation to a culturally diverse community would suggest that Christians from other cultural frameworks are invited, offered hospitality, welcomed, into the Wesleyan congregation where they desire to fellowship. This, in fact, becomes a missional, contextual, response to a culturally diverse neighborhood. Rather than "ghetto-izing" believers of other cultures, all are welcome in the Wesleyan congregation—a powerful symbol of the transformative power of the Christian gospel that breaks down walls.[8]

Choosing monocultural ministry where there is opportunity for multicultural ministry is a way of saying, "We are stronger and more effective separately than together." But this is not the case. Choosing the challenges of multicultural ministry in itself witnesses to the cohesive power of the gospel.

We can show the world what togetherness looks like, togetherness that transcends those who are dissimilar.

Conclusion

In this chapter we looked at what it means to be Wesleyan in our approach to cultural diversity. The fact of God's love, working preveniently, is the basis for pursuing cross-cultural ministry. The fact of God's love at work in a congregation is the power and reason to pursue cross-cultural ministry, and the attitude we have as we approach cross-cultural relationships. When we decisively set ourselves to walk through walls with love, we become a means of grace. The Christian community is the space in which God continues to comfort and empower his people to love, and the space God uses to touch the stranger with love.

Based on this chapter, consider this . . .

- What is the greatest challenge in becoming known and getting to know people of other cultures? Think about language, male-female relationships, social rituals.

- How might these be overcome?

- What is the greatest challenge to loving those whose viewpoints are radically different from the Christian view?

- How can the local church develop a culture of understanding, acceptance and service to those outside the faith?

- We are already on the winning team. God is at work in breaking down walls.

Section 1 Summary

Framework for Multicultural Engagement

In this section, we discussed:

- Ethnic and cultural diversity is a North American sociological reality.
- Diversity is built into God's creation and God's vision of community.
- The church is the means of grace in and through which God communicates his transformative love.
- With a biblical mandate, and a Wesleyan theological stance, we are strategically positioned to make the most of the present opportunity for multicultural ministry.

SECTION 2

ACKNOWLEDGMENT

▲▼▲

How Do We Approach People Who Are Unlike Us?

To acknowledge the right of diverse cultures to live in community we ask:

What do we need to learn about culture?
How can we understand cultural differences?
How can we communicate with cultural sensitivity?

Becoming culturally aware helps us to communicate with respect and openness.

Chapter 5

UNDERSTANDING CULTURAL DIFFERENCES

▼▲▼

Our working definition of multiculturalism is awareness of diverse ethnicities living in the same community, acknowledgment of their right to do so, and commitment to practices of discernment that are condusive to Christian community in which all people can belong.

In this chapter, we briefly explore what we mean by *culture* and how we can become culturally aware.

Understanding our own cultural position helps us become more approachable, and more able to approach people of different cultures.

Culture

When we think of culture, we often have visions of unfamiliar foods, music, art, clothing, and social behaviors. These are indeed cues to help us identify cultural patterns in people groups. But culture is multilayered. These cues are outward indicators of a complex set of responses to the world around us, responses that are so deeply embedded that we are unaware that they are there. Observable patterns within a group are based on shared ideas about the world, a web of beliefs and values—deeply embedded cultural programming—developed over time through human interactions. Thus, culture is a social construct, both corporate and individual. We are shaped by our culture and we influence our culture in an ongoing relational dynamic.[1]

Culture is "the programming that shapes who we are and who we are becoming. It is a social system that is shaped by the individual and that also has the capacity to shape the individual."[2]

Culture is not meant to be a barrier separating people groups, but rather, cultural differences are the gifts we bring to enrich one another. For instance, we enjoy cuisines from all around the world without negating our own cuisine. We acquire new tastes and those different cuisines enhance our own.

This is a metaphor for the way the world's cultures can fruitfully interact. Fundamentally, we are all human; the propagation of cultural groups is a sign of human similarity. Jerry Appleby, Nazarene missionary and cross-cultural ministry expert, points out the fundamental similarity out of which cultural diversity arises: We are universal beings and we share the same basic makeup.

Biologically

"Most scholars argue that the very attempt to divide humans by color (the basis of racial division) is not worthy of discussion. They point out that the stereotyped differences of color, feature, and stature are inconsequential when one notes that human anatomy (including blood types), reproduction, and all bodily functions are primarily the same worldwide."

Intellectually

"Perception, memory, reasoning, emotion, and volition are almost identical among all humans. This is true also of rationalization, projection, attribution, denial, and reaction formation."

Spiritually

"There is a basic need for all individuals to receive and be transformed by the universal gospel. All cultures have some belief and this is a base for all to reach out for the true and living God. A sense of the transcendent, of moral values, of some kind of a symbolic eternity, of explanations for the presence of good and evil are found in all human beings."

We Are Individual Beings

"Every human being is a unique creation of God. Each of us has our own perceptions, feelings, and experiences. There was not, is not, and never will be another that sees thinks, feels, celebrates, or suffers in the identical way. Each of us is a 'one of a kind' human being."

We Are Cultural Beings

"The community, country or culture in which we live shapes every human being. Those who coexist in that community share this combination of values, beliefs, customs, religion, and basic life assumptions that is called culture. Cultures are intriguingly parallel in patterns. Most differences in cultures are in forms of logic, rather than in basic needs."

Culture itself is a universal phenomenon. The instinct to belong and share in a larger narrative is an expression of our humanity. We find our identity in the cultural framework in which we were born. Think about culture as the narrative we share. People groups share other narratives, somewhat similar to ours and somewhat different from ours. In order to relate properly to those with different narratives, we need to develop cultural intelligence.

We can think of cultural intelligence as the ability to relate to, and within, social systems that are different from ours.

Developing cultural intelligence requires that we deconstruct the assumptions we make about other cultures, thereby paving the way for really understanding where other people are coming from.

Cultural Assumptions

Making assumptions that do not accurately reflect reality is a common obstacle to cross-cultural understanding. We all have assumptions about other cultures and other people. Distinguishing between what we think and what actually *is* gives us a level playing field to get to know one another. Oliver Philips, pastor of the Connexions Church of the Nazarene in Lake Como, Florida, and director of the Connexion Empowerment Center Inc., identifies a few common assumptions that we need to deconstruct. This is an important feature of cultural intelligence.

Assumption # 1—All people within a particular culture are the same.

Think about people you know in your own culture. They are unique personalities. The same can be said for other cultures. There really is no blanket "they," as in "they are always talkative, disorganized, creative. . . ." There are creative and uncreative, loud and quiet, organized and disorganized people everywhere. All people groups have personality variances. They may take longer to identify when we are getting to know people from other cultures, and we want to avoid assuming that all people of a culture are like the one person we know!

Assumption # 2—We can be color blind.

Accepting people of other races doesn't mean we are color blind. Thinking that we can, or should, be color blind probably arises from our desires to not be perceived as racially prejudiced. But racial prejudice means we think and behave as though other races are in some way inferior to ours.

To the contrary, racial *awareness* is helpful in understanding others. While racial discrimination dismisses the value of people of another color, racial awareness recognizes, fully accepts, and respects people of all racial origins. Race is an indicator of culture, history, and sociological context. Sensitivity and openness in dealing with other races begin when we recognize and acknowledge racial difference, and we start the process of discerning the unique gifts and perspectives that those of other races bring to the table.

Assumption # 3—America is a melting pot.

By a melting pot, we mean that all differences have merged to produce a homogenous whole. The idea of a homogeneous American culture does not reflect the reality. Instead, what we mean by American culture is the broad outline of prevailing mindsets and a common way of life. But this "big picture" is made up of a mosaic of subcultures, in which various ethnicities continue to operate in their own cultural framework in family and community life. These subcultures are at least double-faceted. The public facet is the way we live in the public sphere, where we seek to fit in, live, and work side by side with others. The private facet is the way we live at home, with families of same origin, the way we eat, our music, our approach to birth, marriage, death, the way we worship. This is the rich mosaic that it is our privilege to discover.

Assumption # 4—Cultural intelligence cannot be learned.

Sometimes people assume that how we see the world cannot and should not change. But changing perspectives is actually a sign of growth. Transformation happens as we renew our minds. Cultural intelligence is developing a perspective and approach to others that reflects our Lord's inclusiveness and acceptance. We can develop our aptitude and strengthen our capacity for interacting with those of other cultures in loving, respectful ways.

Some people are more naturally gifted for cross-cultural work, just as some individuals are more naturally inclined toward engineering, art, or fixing things around the house. But almost everyone can make progress in becoming more effective cross-culturally.

Assumption #5—People from other cultures operate without rational grounds.

We assume this when we do not understand the logic behind certain behaviors. The question should not be about rationality of different behaviors, but about what we need to know in order to understand. Understanding is the ability to see patterns that reveal the values and assumptions that drive behavior.

Assumption # 6—We have a mandate to transform other cultures and eliminate unethical practices.

Here we must tread carefully. The way things look through our own cultural lens may not be the way things really are. Oliver Philips demonstrates the point with this story about *guanxi* in Chinese culture:

Guanxi (gwan-shee) is one of the most powerful forces in Chinese culture. *Guanxi* expresses an obligation of one party to another. More significantly, it expresses an obligation of one person to another over time. *Guanxi* with another person is like a debt owed that will be paid sometime in the future.

The exchange of favors does not have to be in like kind. So, if one person helps introduce you to someone, it is not beyond the scope of the relationship for that party to then ask you to help get a visa to your country, or get their son into a foreign school.

Failure to repay favors in this type of relationship is equivalent to not paying a financial obligation. If one cannot accommodate a specific request, one must find another way to make amends, perhaps by sending along a small gift to let the party know you are sorry you could not help, and that you still want to maintain the relationship.

You can see how Western cultural lens would understand such transactions as bribery. The reality is that *guanxi* is an important social strategy for allowing someone to receive help with dignity, and accept help honorably.

These assumptions arise from interpreting another culture from our own cultural standpoint. Undoubtedly, we each carry around a set of assumptions. Becoming aware of and restructuring these assumptions more accurately paves the way for understanding. Admitting the need for this kind of rethinking is culturally intelligent.

Cultural Self-Awareness

Examining our own culture as a congregation helps us distinguish aspects of our *modus operandi* that are biblically mandated from those that are cultural expressions. Thus, we can identify points where we can be flexible in accommodating other customs and where we must affirm our position with grace and gentleness.[3]

In essentials, unity; in non-essentials, liberty; and, in all things, charity.

To come to this place of cultural competence as a congregation, we need to have honest conversations about what we do and why we do what we do. We need to evaluate how the congregational culture has developed over time, how we influence others and what influences us.

Eric Little suggests these steps toward congregational multicultural competence:[4]

Reality Check

Developing cultural self-awareness means developing insights into where we're coming from, what makes us who we are together. "Churches are communities that organically form by bringing together people with some commonality of tradition, expectation, ideology, theology, and other forms of makeup," says Little.

While this is good and normal, the problem is that we get used to being the way we are, and we are reluctant to change our way of doing things. The existing church congregation almost always expects outsiders to conform to their mannerisms, styles, and polity, because they were here first, they paid for the building, they want to worship a certain way, and they are more comfortable. The existing congregation eschews change in favor of stability.

Cultural competence begins when church leadership honestly admits this state of affairs and becomes, by the help of God, willing to change.

Thus, the first step in self-awareness is to look at how we operate, our preferences, the things that make us anxious, nervous, or afraid. What are the practices that we tend to cling to, that might be challenged by the influence of other cultures in our community?

Mind-Shift

The reality check bears fruit when we look at ourselves and decide that we will change so that God can change others through us. Changing our customs so others will feel at home demonstrates that we are serious about multiculturalism—not far away, where our dollars speak for us, but in our own churches, where we may have to be uncomfortable so that others can be comfortable. A pastor and leadership team should not ask, "How do we think things should be?" but "What can we do to welcome those who need to encounter Jesus?"

Multicultural competency requires that the congregation changes to accept outsiders who have different backgrounds, language, makeup, or worldviews. Not only does a church need to be willing to give up its "sacred cows" and prioritize the gospel, but it must also be willing to alter, change, postpone, or give up practices and traditions that are valid and functional.

How can we move to self-awareness? In a doctoral dissertation, Andreas Dietrich addressed the question of congregational cultural self-awareness. He reviewed cultural models and offered a simple, helpful church survey.[5] Something like this can be of immeasurable value to the church's leadership team.

First Steps

Setting aside our perspectives and preferences and asking what would make us more welcoming produces a series of changes. Little expresses the next steps with clarity—when we start with ourselves, "inwardly examining our churches, and allowing the Holy Spirit to open new doors and possibilities," we will be called upon to make costly, uncomfortable choices:

- We will lose the comfort of playing all of our favorite hymns as frequently as we used to sing them.
- We will not have one language or race represented at our church councils making pivotal decisions.
- We will no longer be able to look upon the potluck buffet and instantly know the ingredients and seasonings in all of the dishes presented.[6]

Self-awareness should lead to a greater sensitivity toward other cultures. Because you know your own tendencies, you now have the sensitivity to move toward something beyond your personal frame of reference.[7]

If we wish to begin including others who are unlike us into our churches, we will have to sacrifice our own identities and lay them at the feet of our Savior Jesus Christ and allow him to re-create us in his beautiful—and multicultural—image.

Putting the interests of others above our own interests is a sign of cultural competence. But it is something more—it is joyful, radical partnership with the Spirit of holy love. It is a small reflection of divine kenosis.

Conclusion

We recognize a degree of ease within our own culture. Words, symbols, and customs are readily understood. But when we think of ours as the only right way, we operate with cultural bias. This approach places the burden of adjustment on others, usually a minority culture.

The way forward in ecclesial culture is to give up the expectation that others need to change, and to choose to be the change we want.

To overcome cultural bias, we need to develop awareness of the web of assumptions, norms, and mores of our particular faith community. Truly acknowledging the right of all people to a place of belonging in our congregations requires that we surrender our own ways.

Based on this chapter, consider this . . .

Start a conversation with your leadership team to develop self-awareness:

- Who are we as a church?

- What are our likes and dislikes in our worship and fellowship?

- Discuss how a person from a different cultural context might feel in our worship service: What might make him or her uncomfortable? Comfortable?

- How do we get past superficial greeting to genuine connection?

- How can we embrace the challenge of cultural inclusion?

- How can we teach our congregation, walk with them patiently, to bring about a new mindset?

Multiculturalism is the acknowledgment of a person's right to belong. Christlike love means we do our best to grant that right where we are and where we can—in our own congregations.

Chapter 6
CULTURAL MODELS
▼▲▼

Cultural self-awareness facilitates the next step in cultural intelligence: Understanding ourselves helps us understand others.

This chapter sketches three cultural models, or types, of broad cultural frameworks. We all tend to fit in one of these. When we learn to identify our, and other people's, framework—the "Where you're coming from"—we can identify points of difference and similarity. This helps us understand others and ourselves in relation to others.

When we do this, apparently perplexing behavior becomes clearer. By understanding cultural context, we can expect great "aha!" moments; we'll be able to smilingly say, "Oh, I get it!" instead of being confused and frustrated in dealing with other cultural groups.

The three cultural models explained here are simply broad sketches of what has become a burgeoning subdiscipline in sociology. Global travel and trade, migration, multinational industrial and economic expansion, and ecclesial mission are only some of the areas in which we need to make culture a basis for, rather than a barrier against, building relationships. These models can help us develop congregational practices that will include a broad range of cultural expressions.

Individual vs. Group

The first model distinguishes between an individual and group framework. While some cultures affirm individual autonomy, others prioritize the community. Soong-Chan Rah in *Many Colors* summarized the distinction[1]:

Individual	Group
Takes individual initiative	Act cooperatively
Makes decisions individually	Make decisions as a group
Nonconformist	Conform to social norm
Puts individuals before team	Put the team before individuals

Valuing individuality means that we operate from our own standpoint, and we expect others to operate from theirs.

Rah explained how group-oriented behavior might appear to the individual-oriented. "On the surface, it may appear that some individuals have developed bad habits or are unnecessarily intrusive and lacking proper boundaries."[2] From a group orientation, being physically and emotionally close is normal. Individual orientation interprets this kind of closeness as invasive. Likewise, those who are operating in an individualistic framework may seem to be "self-involved, insensitive to others or are overly ambitious for personal gain."[3]

When we come to terms with the wide impact of cultural difference we can see the way forward. We can understand how to manage our relationships and become more comfortable with those who do not share our framework. "By identifying the values and motivations under the surface, we are able to suspend judgments and develop cultural intelligence and sensitivity."[4]

Here are simple clues to how these two frameworks may think. You can easily see how different ways of thinking inform different decisions in the same situation.

In an individualistic culture, the mindset might look like this:
"I have to take care of myself."
"I have the right to make my own decisions."
"I can speak for myself."

In a group-oriented culture, the mindset might look like this:
"I belong to my family."
"I am included in this group."
"My choices impact this group."

Knowing the difference between group and individual orientation can help when we're working in multicultural groups.

Think about a pastor who has called a board meeting. When it's time to start, the pastor might go ahead and begin the meeting because she doesn't want to waste the time of those who are already there. This approach suggests the individual model at work—focus on the task, and on the experience of individuals in the group.

But some board members might prefer to wait for those who are probably on their way. These may be more group-oriented. They may think, "We are not all here so we can't start."

Some may prefer to remain ambivalent, leaving the decision to others. They may be somewhere in between, operating in a cultural framework that is neither fully group- or individual-oriented.

Unless these cultural differences are understood, the pastor may seem insensitive, those who want to wait might appear reluctant to get down to business, and those who are ambivalent might appear distanced from the business at hand.

Understanding cultural models helps us discern the group dynamics. When we understand the different perspectives, we might be able to find a more comfortable middle ground. For example, the culturally aware pastor will wait a few minutes and communicate the reason for going ahead without the others, "I'm sure the others will be along shortly, but maybe we can get started so that we don't finish too late." Culturally aware board members might be willing to encourage waiting for a while, but they may also be willing to start sooner than they would have otherwise.

Our discussion here points to opposite approaches. But think of a spectrum, or a range. People can be more oriented to one pole or another. This makes the situation quite challenging, as we may need to spend a great deal of time with others to discern their cultural framework. And we must take care to avoid categorizing others too rapidly or rigidly, because we may operate at different places along the spectrum depending on the situation.

Cultural models give us an idea of what cues to be attentive to, a starting point in the discernment process.

Direct vs. Indirect

One of the most puzzling aspects of working cross-culturally is the difference between the direct and indirect approaches, especially in communication styles.

Accepting and getting used to different cultural approaches sets us up to understand what is being said to us through the words we hear. We can also develop different formulae for social interaction so that others can better understand us.

Direct communication focuses on efficient exchange of information.

DIRECT: "Can you please tell me how to get to Tallahassee."

The speaker states a need and requests help. He or she assumes the response will be either clear directions, or, "Sorry, I can't help you."

But if the question is asked of someone with an indirect approach, the response might be unexpected.

INDIRECT: "I'm not sure . . . Do you have a map?"

From the indirect approach, this is a way of saying "no." But a direct-oriented person would have difficulty understanding this response as a "no," and may even conclude that the person will procure a map and explain the directions.

You can imagine the consternation when this does not play out according to expectations!

How would someone of indirect orientation ask for directions?

INDIRECT: "I'm trying to get to Tallahassee."

The speaker indicates a need, and only requests help by implication, assuming the person addressed will understand that this is a request for help.

DIRECT: "Oh, that's nice. Hope you have a good trip."

The indirect communicator wants to avoid making the direct communicator feel obligated to help. The direct communicator misses this cue, and receives the statement as information sharing. Again, the communication ends in frustration and disappointment for the person needing help, while the person addressed moves on, unaware that he or she disregarded a request for help.

In both examples the situation is easily resolved if we realize that there might be different communication styles. We may come back in the first instance with, "Where can I get a map, please?" and in the second, "Do you know how to get there?"

In neither case do we impose on the other person. We're simply communicating clearly, and seeking more clarity.

Indicators of Indirect Communication[5]

- Priority on feelings and relationships

- Attention to the way things are said
- Concern for how the communication is received
- Avoidance of clear "no" and "yes" type interactions. No might be "not really," "I'm not sure," "I don't think so," "I'll get back to you." Directly communicating a negative might be considered impolite or even insensitive.

Indicators of Direct Communication

- Literal truthfulness
- Efficiency in communication
- Frank communication
- Focus on information
- Engage in conflict

Knowing the mindsets at work behind our interactions informs us as to where we and others are coming from. This awareness allows us to get more from interactions. Tension arises in our relationships when we want different things or appear to want different things. When we understand cultural framework, we can clear the ground for win-win situations.

Task vs. Relationship

In the board meeting referenced earlier, the pastor might be focused on getting through the agenda. When latecomers arrive, the meeting might halt because board members want to greet one another, chitchat about their day, and reveal what happened on their way to the meeting. This may puzzle some who just want to get on with business and consider this small talk a discourteous interruption.

The pastor must understand that there may be a mix of task-oriented and relationship-oriented people in the room in order to navigate the dynamics, to draw the latecomers into the business at hand, and soothe others' frustrations.

Moreover, understanding that more than one cultural model is contributing to the group dynamics can help this pastor develop strategies for a higher degree of both relationality and efficiency. For example, the agenda could be adjusted to address all items and still leave room for the relational dimension.

"In task-oriented cultures, the primary means of achieving one's goals is through skillfully managing tasks and time, whereas, in relationship-oriented cultures the group to which a person belongs is a crucial part of that person's identity and goals are accomplished via relationships."[6]

Here are the key distinctions between these two cultural models:

Task-Oriented	Relationship-Oriented
Focus on keeping good time	Focus on building relationships
Focus on exchanging accurate information	Focus on creating a warm, friendly atmosphere
Define people by what they do	Define people by who they know
Tends toward logical orientation	Tends toward feeling orientation

You can see how frustrating it would be for task-oriented and relationship-oriented people to work together unless they are aware of these differing perspectives. On the other hand, consider the strength of bringing a range of cultural styles to the table. Different perspectives give us a more comprehensive understanding of situations. From our own perspective, we are limited to a single interpretation of reality instead of the whole picture. When we draw together those who have different perspectives, as a result each cultural style enriches and strengthens the whole group.

Merging Disparate Cultural Expressions

These models can be broadly categorized as primary and secondary cultures.

Primary cultures operate within the extended family. They prefer indirect communication and are group- and relationship-oriented.

Secondary cultures operate within the single-family unit, with little connection to the extended family. They are more comfortable with direct, task-oriented, and individualistic modes. Soong-Chan Rah pointed out that the secondary mode is the dominant cultural expression in the United States:[7]

Primary culture is often introduced to immigrants who come from this type of cultural expression in their country of origin. Primary culture, with its emphasis on relationships, may conflict with secondary culture's emphasis on task. Secondary culture's focus on efficiency in communication may contradict primary culture's approach to communication.[8]

Understandably, these two cultures can often come into conflict with each other through misunderstanding of disparate worldviews.

Immigrants to North America may experience deep confusion without realizing the reasons. A congregation that has taken the time to become culturally intelligent can approach displaced individuals with understanding.

The church can develop its own culture—one that reflects cultural sensitivity and inclusiveness. Ecclesial culture can be intentionally shaped for inclusiveness by allowing a broader range of cultural expressions. At the very least, a congregation moving toward cultural diversity would need to come to terms with its existing differences.

Admitting that we are culturally different allows for dialogue that may move us toward understanding our differences and developing norms and customs that more adequately reflect who we are together.

Over time, with perseverance and hard work, we would end up with a third culture that belongs to everyone.

Conclusion

We can work toward developing diverse congregational expressions by developing cultural awareness. This would mean surrendering the cultural expression of only the dominant culture in a congregation. "If the church culture is established in such a way that one expression is valued over another, those coming from a different type of expression will be marginalized, albeit unintentionally."[9]

This is hard work, but the gains are immeasurable. Just think of the church's redemptive impact if lonely, displaced people can come to our church and feel, just for a few moments, that we understand them.

This is a daunting task requiring hard work and ongoing commitment to developing relationships. The more we develop our own cultural intelligence, the more confident we become in guiding our congregations toward understanding other perspectives.

Based on this chapter, consider this . . .

It might be a fun and illuminating exercise to observe these models. Listen and observe:

- Ask yourself what models are being expressed in a conversation.

- How are those models interacting? Do you notice tensions?

- Can you relate the tensions to different cultural models?

This simple exercise is a good place to begin cross-cultural understanding. Meaning is more than words; meaning is the intention behind words; what is being conveyed through what is said and not said.

Chapter 7

CULTURALLY SENSITIVE COMMUNICATION

▼▲▼

We have seen that cultural awareness helps us to locate ourselves in our own cultural narrative—where we're coming from, the lens through which we see the world; the culture of our congregation; and a way to transition to an open and inclusive congregational culture. Developing cross-cultural communication skills is an important way to apply cultural awareness. In this chapter, we consider the question: How can we be culturally aware in social discourse?

Communication in the Spirit of Christ

The rationale for pursuing clear, meaningful conversation is more than its strategic function in developing multicultural communication; it is an expression of who we are as God's people, the God who speaks and gives himself to be known, to call us into fellowship. Reflecting divine initiative, we purposefully learn how to communicate effectively.

God embraced humanity in the incarnation by sending Jesus to become fully human. Bill Selvidge, associate professor of Intercultural Studies at Nazarene Theological Seminary, grounds the principles of effective communication in the incarnation: "Philippians 2:1–11 explains the self-sacrificing nature of Christ's incarnation and encourages all believers to follow Christ's example, gladly giving up whatever rights we may think we have in order to make Christ known to others. Communicating well in the multicultural congregation is an opportunity to reflect grace and to model the spirit of Christ."

We reflect Christ's incarnation by giving up ourselves in order to affirm and care for others through clear messages, both personally and corporately.

Wanting to communicate on the premise of reflecting divine condescension means that we choose to navigate different communication styles. These styles are usually influenced by the cultural framework of origin that we discussed in the last chapter. Being aware of differences is the critical first step in communication. This allows us to comprehend cues that may indicate the cultural framework of our conversation partners. When we are looking for these cues and connect them to the cultural framework, we are likely to experience more effective communication.

Listening

Communicating in the spirit of Christ means putting the other person first; being open and available—it comes down to listening.

Good communication begins with listening to others. Patiently conversing with others sends a significant message: "I value you and want to hear and understand what you say."

Effective listening begins with being interested, with wanting to understand our conversation partner, with wanting to know and be known. Many resources teach us how to communicate effectively, but the bottom line is that we have to want to make connections, to want to do the hard work of learning, practicing, failing, and trying again. And the basis of this desire is the realization that approaching communication in this way is intrinsic to our self-understanding as the people of God.

Meaning and Understanding

The purpose of discourse is to understand and be understood. Our effectiveness largely depends on understanding context, especially cultural context.

What do we mean by context?

If I say, "I'll be right there!" many different meanings can be conveyed:

- If I'm in the next room, "right there" means I'll be there in a moment.
- If I'm in another location, "right there" means I'll come to you as soon as I can get there.
- If someone has already called me a few times, I could mean that I'm getting a little impatient, and I'll be there as soon as I'm available.
- If the context of the conversation is my friend wanting me to watch her play at a concert, I might mean that I'll be right there, perhaps on the front row, eager to see her performance.

In each case, the context of the conversation nuances the meaning of my words. Take this further, and consider how the same words might mean something entirely different if the statement arises from a different cultural context! It follows that we best achieve meaning and understanding when we pay attention to context, cultural context.

When we are from the same area and speak the same language as those around us, we seldom think about how to say what we say; we just say it. In the multicultural congregation, communication quickly becomes a matter requiring our more intense attention.

The challenge is that we draw conclusions about what someone means or we expect others to understand what we mean. This may lead to a communication breakdown. We can walk away from each other with incorrect understandings about the meaning each person was trying to convey. We must approach conversations aware that this can happen and proceed slowly, taking time to verify understanding.

Seeking to Understand

In the multicultural congregation, we aim to fellowship with people unlike ourselves. Communication is our opportunity to reflect Christ's love for others in all we do. The time and effort we put into good communication results in positive regard, good relationships, and a sense of well-being throughout the congregation. We think long-term!

Most of all, yielding our privileges in order to communicate and live out the gospel among others is following our Lord's example.

Gaps of communication exist between us as individuals and groups. We try to bridge these gaps by sending messages that focus on getting the content correct. Once the message is carefully crafted, the communicator may see the task as complete. Yet, our clearest communication may fail to convey the desired meaning unless we consider the other person's frame of reference. We express love when we keep trying to understand, when we seek multiple ways to convey meaning, rather than allowing frustration and communication breakdown to deter us.

Best Practices

What are some of the best practices in communicating for understanding and conveying what we mean?

- Conversations

- Listen
- Be patient
- Give adequate time for communication to be heard and processed
- Repeat as much as necessary, in multiple outlets, and in a variety of ways

Announcements

In messages such as announcements, give at least double the expected time so the hearers may ask questions and clarify what is happening, who is expected to be involved, and who the contact people are.

Verbal messages are the most difficult to understand. Verbal announcements accompanied by their written form give congregants the opportunity to review and clarify for full understanding.

Speaking and writing in simple, direct language communicates most clearly. It is also most easily translatable.

Be inclusive. Be aware of those who may be on the edges of groups either intentionally or because of language difficulties.

Inclusiveness

Take extra effort to be sure that others understand and that you correctly understand their responses. What does "yes" indicate? It may be "I acknowledge that you are speaking to me" or "I agree" or "I understand what you are saying." Learn to understand what a nod or a shake of the head means. An important part of good communication is noticing nonverbal cues.

Learn to see people as individuals and not simply as representatives of a particular ethnic/linguistic/religious group. See beyond the categories (labels) to see the person Jesus loves. Learn and value the cultural ways of various groups. One society may converse and play with children as a way to break down barriers. For others, addressing the eldest person is proper.

Build relationships through fellowship opportunities especially at holidays (your own holidays as well as those of other cultural groups). Invite people to share in meals in host homes.

Invite people to tell their stories, affirming and encouraging those new to the congregation.

And when a problem arises, take responsibility for all miscommunication.

Communicating well begins with the determination to learn and practice good strategies. We never fully master effective communication in our own cultures, let alone across cultures! But we can get better. We can operate with awareness of communication as a conveyor of love.

Cultural Models and Communication

Do we need special skills to communicate well? If so, this is very good news because skills can be learned! Desiring to learn communication skills is half the battle. We soon discover that daily life gives us many opportunities to practice good communication. We can practice being better listeners, keener observers, and more thoughtful speakers in any and all of our everyday social discourses.

As we saw in the previous chapter, knowing the cultural models of conversation partners, their location in the spectrum of direct-indirect, for example, is invaluable for effective communication.

Bill Selvidge remarks, "Communicating well is not simply changing the speed and volume of one's voice, but requires understanding how others communicate and then adapting our way of communication to be truly understood."

So, effective communication is more than speaking the same language; it entails understanding the cultural narratives at work in a conversation. This is particularly important in a multicultural context.

When Communication Breaks Down

In the process of developing communication skills and cultural sensitivity, communication breakdowns will occur. Learning to recognize and repair the breakdown is a valuable skill.[1] Here are three examples of common situations:

Encouraging Participation

Sometimes, in church meetings, we look for everyone to participate. But, participation norms differ greatly across cultures. A multicultural group may represent a range of communication styles, varying from direct and explicit expression of opinions and ideas, to silence and hesitation in expressing thoughts.

How can we facilitate everyone's participation?

The fix: Develop and communicate expectations, for example:

• Go around the table and encourage each person to share.

- Ask open-ended questions.
- Try adopting a "four-sentence" rule to balance between those who love to share and those who hesitate.

Surfacing Disagreement

The way to deal with public disagreement varies across cultures. Individuals from relationship-oriented or group-oriented cultures may favor group harmony over discussing potentially contentious issues.

Those from task- or individual-oriented perspectives may jump right in and engage in conflict, possibly trying to solve a problem for everyone's good. The aim may not be conflict for its own sake, but conflict as necessary to achieve the common good.

Moreover, emotional outbursts are viewed differently in different culture groups: When, for example, people from Latin and Middle Eastern cultures raise their voices, those from more neutral cultures can overestimate the degree of opposition being stated. On the other hand, when others use silence and unreceptive body language to convey opposition, the message is often lost on more emotionally expressive peers.

The fix: To encourage healthy debate, ask everyone to offer pros and cons on a particular course of action so people feel free to argue both sides, without getting locked in to positions they feel obliged to defend.

Giving Feedback

Constructive criticism, while important, can be a sensitive point. The appropriate way to give and receive feedback varies. Individualistic and task-oriented cultures may consider feedback as an opportunity for personal development.

Relationship-oriented cultures may be uncomfortable with giving and receiving criticism directly and formally.

The fix:

- Pastors could work toward a middle ground. For example, work on positive framing for sharing critical feedback.
- Deliver criticisms positively by sharing how things can be done rather than how they're not being done.
- Be open to receiving critical feedback.

Beyond these quick fixes, church leaders can preempt conflict by developing relationships of trust and by taking steps to convey a sense of safety in church meetings so everyone can feel comfortable communicating openly.

Conclusion

We have briefly discussed the need for and basic principles of culturally sensitive communication.

A Christian approach to communication begins with our commitment to reflect God's gracious self-giving. Desiring to connect—persevering, and overcoming our own inhibitions in order to communicate—is an expression of Christlike self-giving love.

On this basis, we can develop our skills through awareness of the range of communication styles that we may encounter in dealing with people of other cultures. This allows us to listen, to communicate carefully, and to verify understanding. We can work through communication breakdown instead of giving up; for to give up on communication is to give up on relationships. We are encouraged to embark on a learning journey that would help us to become increasingly effective in communicating with love and grace.

Based on this chapter, consider this . . .

- What are some challenges in communication that you discern in your conversations?
- Are announcements easy to understand?
- Do you convey information in more than one way?
- How do you know if you're communicating effectively?

Observe reactions to your communication. Notice nonverbal cues for understanding, agreement, puzzlement, and frustration. Become more effective by practicing all the time.

Many resources are available to help you learn to communicate effectively. Some are listed at the end of this book. But even amid frustration, don't give up. Keep learning and practicing. Each of us can benefit from better communication skills. A good communicator focuses on understanding the other person.

Section 2 Summary
Developing Cultural Sensitivity

In this section, we learned:
- Becoming aware of our own cultural framework is the basis for under-standing others.
- Identifying a person's cultural context paves the way for mutual under-standing.
- Effective communication happens when we seek to put ourselves in someone else's shoes by observing, listening, and learning.
- Cultural sensitivity is the process of acknowledging others' right to their own way of being, and seeking to understand our own, as well as other, cultural contexts.

RELATIONAL DISCERNMENT

▲▼▲

What Is God Doing, and What Must We Do?

To develop congregations that welcome the stranger, we ask:

What can we learn from pastors of multicultural congregations?

How can we get to know those who are culturally unlike ourselves?

How can we develop welcoming congregations?

Cross-cultural connections are possible when a congregation chooses to become a place to belong for those who are culturally and ethnically different.

Chapter 8

MOVING WITH
THE HOLY SPIRIT

▼▲▼

Developing multicultural congregations is not an end in itself. It is not aimed at political correctness or being relevant; nor is it a new kind of ministry. Instead, we are convinced that the local church best fulfills its God-given mandate by serving and loving all kinds of people, the entire cultural mosaic of the community it serves.

Like our predecessors, as their story is told in the Acts of the Apostles, we are convinced that we can, and must, be carried along by the Holy Spirit and propelled by the divine energy of holy love. We are compelled to overcome ethnic and cultural barriers and become the means of grace, the redemptive community, the place to belong for individuals of different backgrounds.

The local church has the opportunity to become the parish church, the heartbeat of the community, and a reflection and God-filled expression of the mosaic.

In this chapter, we look at three pastors and their work to develop multicultural congregations. For the most part, the story is told in their own words.

The first scenario is the London First Church, a congregation that became multicultural because it found ways to serve an influx of immigrants to the city. The members of the church did not intend to be multicultural; they intended to serve.

The second is Calvary Church, a congregation that has been transformed from monocultural affluence to vibrant, multicultural relevance.

The third story is about Mosaic Church, a new start that was birthed for multicultural ministry.

Although they operate in different contexts with different types of congregations, these three stories have some common themes: God-given vision, response to community need, and the congregation's willingness to change.

"Once you know where God is working, you can adjust your life to join him," authors Henry T. Blackaby and Claude V. King point out in *Experiencing God.*[1]

Congregational Growth through Community Service

London First Church of the Nazarene
London, Ontario
Pastors: Rev. Junior and Rev. Rose Sorzano

Twenty-two years ago, when we accepted the call to this church, the congregation was primarily Anglo-Saxon Canadian with a few families of other nationalities. We did not set out to develop a multicultural ministry. But the demographics of London were changing, and if we wanted a thriving congregation and ministry, we had to come to terms with the changing cultural landscape. I believe that divine will and the congregation's desire to minister to the needs of our community precipitated our growth as a multicultural church.

My wife and I are from the Caribbean, and I think this "face" of the church sent a message that we were open to people from many cultures. Our move to multicultural ministry was jump-started at the conjunction of two events:

1. An influx of Hispanic people filled our community, and we began to pray about how we could minister to them.

2. Around the same time, at the Church of the Nazarene 2001 General Assembly mission convention, God spoke to my heart about planting another local church in London.

In response to a very evident need, and conviction of God's leading, I returned from the General Assembly and started to make some connections. I spoke to Mary Wallace, a former Latin American missionary, about leading a Bible study for the three Hispanic families attending our church at that time. I also contacted Rev. Pedro Fernandez, one of our Spanish pastors and shared my vision for Spanish-language ministry. Pedro also had a vision to plant churches. He brought a leadership team to London, and we began to have services with a couple from his congregation. Lucy and Alberto Majestre came weekly from Toronto to lead this new ministry.

The weekly Bible study and Saturday evening service began to grow and resulted in the Spanish congregation that today is independent of the mother congregation. Some of the Spanish families decided to remain in our English congregation, preferring our ethnic diversity.

God prepared the way for us, and we simply moved along with his leading.

Over time, our church became an open door to people from all classes of society—we became multicultural and multigenerational. Now we have practices that have become a part of who we are, for example, once a quarter we have "International Sunday" when we celebrate our diversity and share a meal with food from various ethnic cultures.

We include songs and scripture in different languages in our services.

As a result, our fellowship is like a foretaste of heaven where people of all cultures, ethnicities, generations, and classes will dwell together as one. It is the beauty of the lion and the lamb existing in community.

As a result of our experience and ministry, I have learned these important principles for establishing and sustaining a multicultural local church:

Intention: It's not about becoming multicultural, but about engaging with people from other cultures.

Attention: We need to be attentive to those who live on our doorstep.

Our church provides services such as ESL classes, cross-cultural services, free clothing giveaway, and a food pantry. We intentionally sought to understand and meet their needs. This helped us to make connections, those connections led to relationships, and relationships led to congregational growth.

Process: It takes time and effort to develop multicultural ministry.

Once we recognized that God was leading us into multicultural ministry, we aimed to become multicultural rather than to simply do multicultural ministry. We realized that we had to be sincere about developing relationships and building bridges with people of other cultures. We learned to respect them. We did not seek to change them and make them culturally like us.

Systematic: It is necessary to learn cultural sensitivity.

We had to make a choice to become culturally aware in order to establish lines of communication.

The parable of the Good Samaritan (Luke 10:25–37) illustrates that we must overcome cultural and social barriers to meet our neighbor's needs. The priest and the Levite did not seize the opportunity to go beyond social, cultural, and racial norms. Pursuing multicultural ministry is like being the Samaritan. It requires seeing past differentness, recognizing common humanity, and responding with love.

What do we notice in the London First story? A pastor and congregation with missional hearts—they just wanted to make disciples, and the cultural origin of potential disciples did not present a barrier, only a challenge.

Here is what they did, and it worked:

- They prayed for God's vision, direction, and provision.
- They identified and responded to concrete needs.
- They offered people the opportunity for worship and fellowship in their own language.
- They were open to multicultural worship.
- They developed cultural awareness and prepared themselves to communicate with people.

Implementing these strategies takes time, persistence, prayer, and working together. So this is not only a missional/outreach opportunity but also a means of unifying and strengthening the existing congregation.

Challenge? Yes. But challenge and opportunity always coexist.

Choosing Multiculturalism

Calvary Church of the Nazarene
Annandale, Virginia
Pastor: Rev. James and Rose Heyward

Now, we look at another ministry context: a monocultural congregation that has chosen to become multicultural. When James and Rose accepted the call to Calvary Church about twelve years ago, this was a monocultural, affluent congregation. But their community, just outside Washington, D.C., is multicultural. The journey has included developing a congregational culture that would make the church accessible and welcoming to the community.

Like Junior, James recalls a specific experience God used to call him to pastor a multiethnic church, a call that God has continued to affirm over the years. This affirmation has shaped his approach to ministry. Another shaping influence is his conviction that God intends for us to use our gifts and for us to be ourselves in our ministry context. God has used James's gift of bringing people together to develop this congregation.

James shares these principles about his church's journey to diversity:

Mission: Where are we going?

The church has to exist in and embrace a diverse community. The question of where we are going must be answered for us to arrive at the desired destination. Churches move from monocultural to multicultural on purpose. Embracing and seeking to reflect the community's cultural makeup must be a driving passion and value of church leadership and the congregation.

The mission of being a multicultural church has to be reflected in all aspects of the church's identity, branding, leadership, and ethos.

Message: What's being said?

The message has to be one of truth and justice, *not* the American way. Our American ideas of politics and economics are challenged in a multicultural community. Mosaic is not the natural ethic of American society. The church is called to be the prophetic voice crying in the wilderness.

How we deal with current issues such as immigration, crime and punishment, poverty, and race become important markers as to whether or not we value diversity as actuality rather than ideology.

Minister: Who is visible?

The makeup of church leadership is important in the move from monocultural to multicultural. People like to see "themselves" represented in the church. Nothing sends a louder message about commitment to diversity than the faces on the stage.

A church trying to be more inclusive needs to reevaluate the makeup of its staff, lay leadership, and ministry teams.

Melody: What do we sing?

The church needs to sing one message through many styles. The main musical style must be evaluated for crossover potential. The main style serves as an entrée, while leaving plenty of room for other musical flavors. As different cultures are represented in the congregation, those musical styles can be added to the main course of music.

Monitor: What's the cost?

In moving toward congregational diversity, church leaders will face criticism, loss of reputation, and deeply rooted traditions. Some of the congregation may express desire for diversity, but may actually have great difficulty with the changes required by such a commitment. Leaders may see the departure of some, but may also be able to walk with the congregation into more acceptance of, and willingness to, change.

Although it may be costly, as the church embraces this mission, the neighborhood will see what God can do through his people—the living reality of the kingdom of God on earth through the reconciliation of races and interweaving of cultures.

Change has been the greatest challenge for this pastor and congregation. They have changed the physical appearance of their worship space. Their sanctuary was built in the traditional style, but this distanced the people they were trying to reach. They had to ask, "How does the church look to others?" and "What does the building say about what kind of church we are?"

They have been willing to undergo the discomforts of change in order to send a welcoming message to the community.

One example of change is the Tapestry Café they started. James tells the story:

> In an attempt to help people understand us as a worshipping community and our mission of embracing the multicultural ethnic community around us, I initiated three changes to our worship auditorium. The first was to include a café (Tapestry Café) in the auditorium. I believed that connecting is an important aspect of being a multiethnic community. This was the motivation for the café. This idea was not as well received as I expected, for many reasons including cost, and, well, no one puts a cafe in the worship auditorium. But we persisted with the idea because we believed a café in our worship space would send a message that connecting was important and that we were a different type of church.

James also tells us about introducing international flags into the auditorium:

> We hung international flags from the mezzanine of the auditorium. Each year we would unfurl flags from some of the 156 world areas where the Church of the Nazarene is present for our Faith Promise weekend. After the weekend, we rolled them back up for safekeeping until the next

event. After the Faith Promise celebration four years ago, I suggested that the flags in our auditorium sent a wonderful visual message of who we were and wanted to become.

Another creative auditorium change was to commission and include local art representing many ethnic cultures.

These three changes were not met with widespread acceptance. When I floated the idea of the café some felt it was too expensive, too out of the box, and too nonspiritual. After all, who eats in the sanctuary? My own staff and wife even gave me the "Are you crazy?" stare as I discussed plans for a café in the auditorium.

I remember well the day a young lady came to me and said that people were not supposed to eat in the sanctuary; that it was a sin. I said I didn't think it was a sin to eat in church and that opinions change over the years.

We pushed through and decided that the café was important to help folks understand our community and mission. Today, that young lady and her parents lead the hospitality team that helps people connect around the table as they eat doughnuts and bagels and drink coffee in the auditorium.

The international flags and ethnic artwork faced some opposition as well. But, I had learned from the café situation that my job was to help the community of faith see what it could not see—a multiethnic community of faith connecting in a place where everyone would feel comfortable and included.

The newest change that we have made as a community of faith is in our worship service. We call it The Gathering, an experience that is:

Experiential

Participatory

Image-rich

Connective

The Gathering Experience flows from connection to response:

- Intentional connecting—around the table through food, announcements, updates, and time of greeting.
- Worship—through instrumental and vocal music, multimedia presentations, scripture reading, and a message from God's Word.

Response to God through:

1. Singing,

2. The Eucharist,

3. Tithes and offerings, and/or

4. Praying at an altar with or without assistance.

5. Reflection and application—an opportunity to make connections between The Gathering and living between Sundays.

The Gathering was met with some skepticism and opposition. To help us make a softer transition, I did "Pie with the Pastor." This gave me the chance to explain how The Gathering would help us better connect and be more open to new folks.

After two delays, we launched The Gathering last year and it was an instant success.

The key:
- Stick with the vision.
- Develop strategies.
- Make decisions based on the vision.

▼▲▼

Multicultural New Start

Mosaic Church of the Nazarene
Florence, Arizona
Pastor: Rev. Kevin and Lisa McGinnis

The Mosaic Church is committed to a culture of inclusiveness: "Our doors will be open to all in a blending of ages, races, and musical styles. We will be a mosaic whose beauty and service will be revealed as each diverse part makes us more complete while we serve our Maker."

Through his own experience, Kevin identified the essential principles that have been fruitful in starting a multicultural congregation.

Calling

The first step in the life of the church planter is knowing and embracing a true calling and love for the people in his or her parish. The person needs a God-given sense of "mantle" or "burden" for the specific people he or she wants to reach, much as it is for those who leave their own countries and begin mission work abroad.

Self-awareness
- How aware are you of your own cultural perspective?
- How has your life experience shaped the way you see your community?
- How does this affect how you minister to your parish?

- Would your worldview allow you to understand and minister to anyone not like you?
- What steps do you take to look beyond your own cultural mindset?

For effective cross-cultural ministry, we have to be capable of taking the approach expressed in these words of Phineas Bresee: "On the great fundamentals we are agreed. Pertaining to things not essential to salvation, we have liberty. An unwillingness for others to enjoy the liberty that we enjoy in reference to doctrines not vital to salvation is bigotry, from which the spirit of holiness withdraws itself."

Know Yourself

Connect with someone you trust who can mentor you in this self-discovery and can equip you for the task of missional parish ministry.

Good Theology

Good theology is essential to ministry, but especially when you're encountering others from a myriad of cultures and religious backgrounds. You will encounter many with worldviews that do not resemble yours. Get to know what other faiths believe. Know what you believe. Work, study, and prepare yourself so you can reach the people of your parish.

Prayer and Word

Be so very intimate with your Maker that you recognize his voice and respond as Abraham did. God spoke; Abraham acted. Pray so that you are "ready in and out of season" (2 Tim. 4:2, CSB, ESV, NASB). Bathe all you do in prayer. Be in an attitude of prayer all day. In constant communion with God, we receive the power, love, and passion, the sense of urgency without which ministry is not possible.

A Team

Gather a team of devoted holiness lay ministers around you. A call to a new mission field or parish is affirmed if the saints you know will partner with you in prayer, in talent, and in resource. Who will see the mission and devote themselves to it? A new church start begins pretty small. Let it begin with those who share your call.

Go!

Abraham is our great example. God said go, and Abraham went. Go and be used for a season. Be open to the idea of "adventure" as a positive thing. Be prepared to invest all of you into it.

Share

Sharing this call, if you are married, is nonnegotiable. This is a family affair, and if you have children, they, too, will share in this "adventure." Let the call be a source of enrichment for the family.

Connect

Look for any way to get involved. Introduce yourself and your strengths to the leadership of your town. Join the chamber of commerce. Meet the leaders of the local Boy Scouts and Girl Scouts. Meet the police chief, fire chief, sheriff, the mayor, the town or city council. Share your gifts and skills in community service.

- Where does your community gather?
- What public clubs are available?
- What service organizations are there?
- Is there a community resource center you can connect with—a pregnancy center, tutoring center, or recreation department?
- What community events draw all of the different cultures in your parish?

Stretch yourself; learn names and use them. Know your restaurant servers; ask about their families. Know the teachers and staff at the local schools and community centers, adult care facilities, and hospitals. Meet the local teachers and education directors.

It's not as much a "build it and they will come" but a "go unto all the world."

How best can you promote the kingdom of God in your parish?

- Love your people.
- Think of yourself as the parish pastor.
- Behave as if you are called to everyone.
- Live as if everyone you meet outside the church will know Jesus because of your and your congregation's faithfulness.

Build Out

Begin additions to the ministry only as you have the team who can do these with excellence. As the congregation grows and you discover the members' strengths, you can address more and more areas of need in your parish.

In what creative ways can you reach the many different people in your community? What are some felt needs as well as obvious needs your parish has?

Vision

- Keep the vision and the mission before the congregation.
- Teach as if the congregation is a reflection of the community, a reflection of all cultures.
- Remind your people of the Master's mandate to make disciples of all nations.

We are surrounded by so many people who need the answer of the gospel in their lives. How wonderful is it when we begin to see a congregation look like its community!

Kevin tells the story of how these principles have borne fruit in his ministry:

I have been blessed to serve in a small town of 26,000 people. We are a prison town, and 18,000 of our 26,000 are incarcerated. Our congregation includes people from different cultures, and certainly, each one has a unique story: the ex-con, the prostitute rescued from sex-trafficking, the professor of science contributing to NASA's space program, the inventor of the modern airbags, teachers, administrators, managers, laborers, retirees, sheriff deputies, correctional officers, town council members, the list goes on and on. We gather as a microcosm of God's Kingdom here on earth.

What beauty is present on Sundays as we gather to worship together!

Serving as the head lifeguard in our town has been a great way to get to know people. When they get to know me as a lifeguard and then come to church and meet me as pastor, they are already predisposed to being a part of our church. Often, I get curious looks from new people. I get this a lot:

"Pastor, I have been trying to place you. Where have we met before?"

Often, I already know their names and their kids' names. So it goes something like this:

"Mike, we have met at the Watermark; I taught Bryan to swim last month. I'm the head lifeguard!"

And they respond with, "Oh! Kevin! Ha, ha, ha! Yes! I'm sorry; I didn't recognize you with clothes on!"

Our mission is to reach people for Jesus not only on Sundays, but every day, and everywhere. For several months, I visited a young man in one of our prisons. When he was released on probation, he was excited to meet me face to face, and he approached me with a smile. As he bent over from his great height of 6'4" to shake my hand (I am 5'5"), he said, "Pastor Kevin! It's Bobby! You're a little pastor!"

I said, "You're a giant! I'm so glad you're here today!

"Where do I sit, Pastor?"

"Right inside and to your left. Find a seat anywhere you like. I'll see you inside."

Bobby found a seat on the back row, not far from Sherry and Randy. After a while, he turned to Randy:

"I'm sitting here and trying to figure out how I know you? Have we met before?"

And Randy, with a big smile, said, "Yes, Bobby we have met. What are you doing out already? I just arrested you a few months ago."

Bobby, suddenly very uncomfortable, responded, "Oh! yes, Deputy! Yes sir, maybe I should sit somewhere different."

Sherry turned to Bobby with a kind smile.

"Bobby, you will do no such thing! You two will get along just fine, and you will sit by us each week. The ground at the foot of the cross is level. You are always welcome here!"

Today, almost six years later, Bobby has committed his life to Christ. He has met a Christian lady and they are very happy together. They were married on a Sunday morning at our sister church in Phoenix a few months ago.

This is the kind of love and acceptance that can make a church a real place to belong for everyone. Connect with people: Keep vision and passion alive, and pray.

Conclusion

This chapter has put us in touch with the "happening" of multicultural ministry. The story behind these examples is one of God-given vision, passion, commitment, and a congregation with a missional heart. In each case, we have seen that challenge accompanies opportunity; that God is at work, preparing the hearts of people; and that the church is called to be incarnational, to be the means of grace to convey Christ's love.

Based on this chapter, consider this . . .

- What needs in your community might be a catalyst for launching into multicultural ministry?

- What message does your worship space send to your community?

- How would you answer Kevin's questions about your community?

- How can you and your congregation become more visible to people of other cultures?

Chapter 9

CULTIVATING COMMUNITY CONNECTIONS

▼▲▼

In the previous chapter, we saw the importance and fruitfulness of getting to know our neighbors, and of identifying and responding to specific needs. In this chapter, we take a closer look at how to develop these relationships, the nuts and bolts, and the concrete spaces in which we can apply cultural sensitivity and express love through service and friendship.

Relationships are the means through which the love of God can touch the hearts of people. Without relationships, our community service loses its missional dimension and redemptive impact. Without genuine connection, we risk becoming a social service entity instead of the love-filled church of Jesus Christ.

In this chapter, we look at developing genuine friendships. Friendships can occur as we get involved in community building, discussed in the second section of this chapter. Finally, we look at how hospitality can bring the community together and promote meaningful relationships.

Person to Person

Connecting with someone at a meaningful level is a source of deep happiness. We build relationships through commitment and hard work. But we are often reluctant to risk being open to others. Undoubtedly, if we are serious about developing strong relationships, we risk being vulnerable, put ourselves out there, make overtures to someone without being sure of the response.

Friendship

Being a friend is the test of our capacity to love, and the demonstration of the power of God's love flowing through us. We, on our own, are compelled to protect ourselves, put up walls, keep connections superficial, and certainly, remain within the more comfortable space of relationships with like-minded people.

But by the powerful grace of God we shed our protective skin, become truly human, and choose fellowship.

Unless we choose this openness, we approach others on false terms. We seek a position of power, the position of needing nothing, presenting ourselves as invulnerable. This position keeps us safe, keeps our walls up. But friendship is a risk. Always. It is an even greater risk when we have to navigate through cultural differences to clear the ground and connect with someone. This takes time.

The end game in reaching out to others is to share the love of Jesus. It may seem that serving others, meeting their needs, is how we show love. And this is certainly a way to show we care. But if our connection to others is only at the level of meeting needs, if our connection is no real connection at all, but a mere impersonal handout, we really have no opportunity to truly convey God's love. Instead, God's love is demonstrated at the point of genuine friendship.

The best way to start is to start. Take a risk and reach out to someone in friendship, not to say something, not to fix anyone, not for any other agenda besides the desire to connect with someone, to be human.

Take baby steps. Test the waters. Persist. Practice cultural sensitivity.

Approach relationships intending to get to know the other and to disclose yourself. A relationship is an exchange of personhood, knowing and being known. Wanting to fix someone, wanting to be right, are obstacles to genuine reciprocity. We must begin the journey by extending the hand of fellowship with the intention, "I want to know you. I want you to know me."

Storytelling

As friendship develops, it brings opportunity for redemption, for healing, and for wholeness. What do I mean? As we journey together with increasing trust and intimacy, we get a chance to share ourselves. We can listen to each other's stories. Stories can often be intended to convey information, or to push through a certain agenda. Stories can give shades of meaning to veil the truth. We share our story to give information about ourselves. We can also share a story to convey our feelings. But storytelling allows us to really connect with one another.

The real power of story is that it discloses identity. And this is where the real conversation happens. But these levels of conversation must be pursued over time. This is part of the process of building friendship. These kinds of conversations are not about who is right, but about what we can learn from and about one another. A learning conversation happens when we feel safe and accepted, and we can open up about who we really are.

If a learning conversation is about self-revelation and attempting to communicate identity, then in effect, a learning conversation is the art of storytelling. Storytelling is the ultimate self-disclosure. It reveals insights into the personality, emotions, content, and identity of the individuals. It requires self-disclosure while presenting a way to move the conversation forward.[1]

Tell the truth, share pain, share who you are. Take the risk of being vulnerable. Stories have the power to build and develop community on multiple levels.

Lament

Certainly some stories exist that we don't want to tell and others we don't want to hear. But friendships will eventually come to this point. And, despite the discomfort and pain, "in the process of developing a multiethnic community and creating an environment conducive to multicultural ministry, there has to be a willingness to hear each other's stories and learn through conversations with one another."[2]

The reason some stories are hard to tell or hear is that they are accompanied by pain. What do we do? Do we drop our eyes and change the subject? Do we get uncomfortable and back away. Do we introduce space into the relationship because we really don't want to "go there"?

But at this point of risk, the love of Christ compels us to press forward for the sake of love, thereby allowing something extraordinary to happen, for someone to encounter the love of Christ through us. We can choose to hear the painful story and share the painful story.

Storytelling in Christian fellowship opens the way for lament, and lament allows for deep healing. In a diverse community, there will be those who have been marginalized because of being different. Issues of race come up. We get to choose if we'll keep our relationships superficial, or if we will risk opening up to each other. We determine if we'll insist on being the kind of church community where people are safe, where people can be vulnerable, where stories can be told, and where the community can join the lament with the broken.

This is an important expression of Christ's love. We become a community of different people bound together with shared pain. The binding together that arises from shared pain is itself the way to healing, the binding up of the broken heart.

Think about how powerful the church's witness becomes when we take the call to love seriously, personally, and in ways that will change us, challenge us, and transform us.

In his insightful book, *A Fellowship of Differents: Showing the World God's Design for Life Together*, Scot McKnight made this compelling claim about the identify of Christian community:

The church is God's world-changing social experiment of bringing unlikes and differents to the table to share life with one another as a new kind of family. When this happens, we show the world what love, justice, peace, reconciliation, and life together are designed by God to be. God designed the church to make the previously invisible visible to God and to one another in a new kind of fellowship.[3]

When we create a safe space for stories, for exchange, for lament, for sharing tears and pain, joy and laughter, we embody the love of Christ in visible ways. A community that can lament is a community that brings reconciliation.

Love is messy. Love is hard work. Love is fellowship. Let's dream dreams and see visions of how a community of redemptive connections can heal, break down walls, and bring in a new day where "unlikes" are loved and "differents" are different together.

Community Involvement

We get involved in the community by identifying a need, giving our service, and developing a strategy—or responding. This is not trying to fix people. It is more like putting people on track in a way that empowers them. It is collaboration with community members to build a stronger community together. This may well be a costly venture—involvement sometimes requires that we share our resources.

Working to make life better for our neighbors will demand thoughtful, prayerful reconsideration of how we use our resources. Jerry Appleby remarks: "If we want to change the communities in which we live, the church of Jesus Christ must become serious about sharing the resources that God has blessed us with. This is basically a call to live in the community of goods that arose almost intuitively under the power of the Holy Spirit in the New Testament church."

This means churches may have to redistribute resources in the interests of the community. Taking this direction may lead us to ask ourselves questions such as, "How does this contribute to our mission?" and "How can we make life better for people in our community?"

Love means we give ourselves away, and giving ourselves away may mean using our resources for others, where perhaps we may not immediately see how giving may positively impact church attendance. We have many resources to help us develop community ministries that are healthy and sustainable, that promote the well-being and flourishing of the community.

Community development is challenging. We need to be cautious about taking over and fixing the problems of families and communities. Respectful collaboration requires working with our community partners, allowing the community to set the pace, while we maintain the position of serving, even though we may be making the greatest contribution financially and otherwise.

But as we work side by side with the families in our neighborhoods, we may be able to make the connections that will eventually lead to lasting friendships.

Hospitality

Hospitality is necessary to build bridges between individuals of different cultures. People may come to church and find it difficult to connect. But everybody has to eat, and food is a critical part of culture. Food can become a point of conversation to begin establishing a connection between people. Sharing a meal is a fundamental, universal way of expressing belonging. A shared meal is "the one place that consistently provides the place of connection and community. . . . Besides good conversation, there is something significant about sharing the intimate moment of consuming a meal. Even if the congregants speak different languages, they can still effectively communicate by sharing culture through the expression of food. . . . Some of the best moments in the life of a multiethnic church are in the sharing of meals."[4]

Sharing meals is a great starting point to express hospitality, but deep connections must be encouraged to flourish through fellowship and community involvement.

Friendship, community development, hospitality—not simple or easy; but possible. These strategies will, over time, transform a congregation into a fellowship that welcomes different people from all walks of life.

As Soong-Chan Rah says, "The church is not merely a place where we tolerate strangers; it is a place of grace and acceptance that comes from being a family."[5]

Conclusion

In this chapter, we have seen that the skills of cultural intelligence and culturally sensitive communication bear fruit in deep friendships. The love of Christ compels us to risk friendship. The fellowship of believers can become a space of safety and acceptance, where our shared stories can be heard, where pain can be acknowledged so that healing can begin. The church is called to be a family. This is the great adventure to which God calls us.

Based on this chapter, consider this . . .

- What expressions of friendship, community involvement, and hospitality are available to you and your church now:

  What individuals might need a friend?

  What can the church do to serve and empower the community?

  How can you encourage hospitality in your congregation?

Take the risk. Start small. Take baby steps. Keep going.
Pray for the person you want to be friends with.

Chapter 10
WELCOME AND WORSHIP
▼▲▼

The previous chapter dealt with building cross-cultural relationships. In this final chapter, we come to the important matter of worshipping together.

How do we navigate the ways of worship that are meaningful and important, but so deeply different from culture to culture?

The dominant culture in a congregation tends to cling to "doing worship" their way, mainly because the majority sees a certain way as the right way. Over time, custom gets enmeshed with genuinely biblical and theological grounds.

The unvoiced expectation is that "new people can and should adjust to the way we do things here." But Sunday morning in North America is a great opportunity to visibly demonstrate the power of Christ's love to bring all kinds of people together.

If we're serious about becoming a space of belonging, we may have to surrender some of our most cherished traditions. This is a challenge and opportunity—a challenge because change is difficult; opportunity because the dominant culture gets to publicly express self-giving love, to give up its ways in favor of a smaller group.

Sadly, sometimes a dominant culture is unwilling to change the appearance of its sanctuary, its mode of worship, or its particular ways and customs. In such a congregation, people from other cultures are guests, even honored guests, but not family.

In this chapter, we think about how commitment to become a family of "differents"—where all kinds of people have a voice, a right to participate fully in worshipping the one God—can be put into action. We explore how we can display grace and love by surrendering our preferences and working toward a new culture that reflects the congregation's diversity.

The truth to which we must insist on being faithful is this: We want to worship God. Together.

What really matters is God's response, his delight in the worship we give him.

Right away this relegates our "sacred cows" to last place. While it is important that all feel a sense of belonging, the anointing of the Holy Spirit, his presence, enables true worship, and creates and strengthens the unity of the church.

Welcoming Space

The delightful story of Calvary Church's Tapestry Café demonstrated how we can employ existing space in bold, new ways to produce a warm, welcoming area. There is no one right way to create welcoming space. It is a matter of letting go of how we like our sanctuary to look, thinking about how it may appear to others, and working together to introduce arrangements that send a welcoming message.

The main concern is to step outside ourselves in order to see from someone else's perspective. Take, for example, this reaction from first-time visitors to a local church: "It was really daunting as I walked up. I didn't know which door was the main entrance."

How easy is it for people to walk into our church off the street?

Think about if your space is entirely Western/American in appearance. Are there flags of other nations, or just the American or Canadian flag? Consider what is on the platform. Are there any musical instruments that are not Western?

Atmosphere

But space is more than architecture and physical symbols. It is also atmosphere. How might people feel when they come in?

"I was early. While I sat there, a couple of people talked; the music team set up at the front. No one paid attention to me and the activity was distracting."

How ready are we to receive new people? How do we draw newcomers into feeling ready to be a part of the worshipping community?

Welcome

And then, there's the way we greet people who are different in appearance, who may not be dressed in our Sunday norm.

"Someone greeted me, but after that, I was left to myself. I sat at the back and tried to be inconspicuous. I tried to make eye contact with people, but they smiled, then looked away."

How might new people feel when they come in?

"After the service, I felt awkward. No one came to talk to me. I hurried away as soon as I could. But the service was great."

How Attentive Are We to Visitors?

"Everybody was wearing jeans and sandals. We put on our best for church. I felt overdressed."

Would the way we dress make people feel uncomfortable?

These are challenging questions because we are comfortable with our customs, and customs are hard to change. We take them for granted, and we tend to not reflect on how others see us.

Lynn Nichols, pastor of Northside Church of the Nazarene in Watauga, Texas, explains, "Culture dictates how we dress when we come to church, greet visitors, sing, pray, study the Word, take communion, and structure our ministry. Unless challenged, our cultural traditions are often mistaken for gospel, and as a result they are defended as gospel."

Worship and Preaching

Worship in the multicultural congregation typically includes the same components as in monocultural services: prayer, singing, Scripture, preaching, and may also include greetings and responses, and passing the peace of Christ. Worship leaders need to intentionally plan and conduct the service in ways that draw the whole congregation into worshipping God together.

Such planning is receptor-oriented, asking, "How will worshippers understand this?"

The enrichment that comes from a multicultural congregation far outweighs the adjustments made.

Bill Selvidge shares these insights: "Few practices are as personal as worship, involving our minds, hearts, emotions, and certainly language. Worship is a corporate event, an experience of meeting God together with other believers."

In the multicultural congregation people worship in ways they have learned in their various cultures. For worshippers who are new to Christian faith, the whole worship experience may be totally unlike anything they are familiar with.

It is important to be sensitive to these different perspectives. It is important for congregational leadership to develop sensitivity that is more than an emotional, sentimental instinct, but is a commitment to view things from the stranger's perspective.

Ask questions such as:

- How does this person feel, what is this person's experience here?
- How can we communicate that we ardently desire to have this person worship with us, and become one of us?
- How grateful are we that a new someone has come to worship with us, and how much are we willing to bend to make that happen?

I can't overstate the importance of leadership that sets this agenda. We cannot expect people to come into our church and adjust to our ways.

Language

If the main language of the multicultural service is English, both Scripture reading and musical lyrics are challenging for non-English speakers. Formal Bible translations may use vocabulary that is above the level of many English language learners. Paraphrase translations may be based on certain cultural assumptions the learners may not understand.

Printed material on the screen or in bulletins would be helpful. For example, the Overland Park Church helps their large group pf Chinese by displaying on the screen the Chinese translation of the Scripture passage being read in English. The Grand Rapids West church provides everything in Haitian Creole and English for its bilingual congregation. San Bernardino First bilingual church produces Spanish/English bulletins and displays songs and scriptures in Spanish and English.

Music

Historically, hymns have helped worshippers to praise God as well as teaching important doctrines of the faith. However, hymns may also be written in vocabulary with unfamiliar historical references.

How can we help multicultural congregations share the richness of these musical forms that have moved generations of worshippers with deep, holy ecstasy? This is an ongoing challenge. Attention to clear, simple lyrics is a good place to start, especially as this would facilitate translation.

Multicultural congregations may find that a range of various types of music and in the languages of congregants is most conducive to meaningful corporate worship.

For instance, "A church that desires to reach out to a nearby refugee community will need to give up a significant portion of its current playlist in favor of music that truly allows that community to worship. And the church will need to do so with joy and willingness to see and hear the gospel message retold in Swahili, Arabic, Quechua, or whatever that language may be, despite the fact that congregants don't understand it at all."[1]

Music carries evocative power. It touches our emotions, is embedded in our memories, and is deeply personal. Changing what we sing and how we sing is significant for a congregation. We can overcome our own misgivings by being empathetic with those from other cultures. They have left everything that is familiar. They are experiencing culture shock, trying to understand and function in an entirely new environment. Many feel exiled. If we look at the situation from their perspective, we can more easily work through these changes, and be encouraged. Think about how appealing displaced people would find a worship experience that includes elements that are familiar to them.

Leadership

As the church pursues multiculturalism it ends up developing its own culture. Being visible in the community, developing relationships, and sending a strong welcoming message—over time, these strategies bear fruit. When this happens, everyone rejoices.

This brings the congregation to another challenging step: In order to sustain multiculturalism, local church leadership needs to be drawn from the ethnic makeup of the congregation. Regarding the music team, ushers, Sunday school teachers, board members—we must ask, "How many are of the dominant culture, and how many are of other ethnicities?"

If the dominant culture is still in the majority across the board, we must ask, "Why aren't more cultures participating?"

Usually, the default position in local church leadership is for the same people to continue in the ministry positions they've held for years, because they know how, they've always done it, and we are reluctant to rock the boat.

It is more of a challenge to identify, train, and mentor newer people for leadership positions. But we must accept this challenge to assure sustainable multiculturalism.

Tom Nees, former director of USA/Canada Mission and Evangelism, remarks, "Denominations need to adopt strategies to encourage mission outreach and church development within all people groups. At a minimum, that means recognizing and supporting leaders of groups underrepresented within the denomination. Denominational events, boards, and conferences need to be carefully managed to include diverse participants."

Denominational events should reflect not only their present diversity but their desired diversity. Ethnic minority groups will want to see representatives from their communities at the table in decision-making roles as well as on the platform in public denominational events. While individual congregations may not necessarily look like America, Canada, or even their surrounding neighborhoods, denominations with all their diversity can come closer to the ideal of reaching and including all the people groups of society.

Commitment to diversity is a missional response to ethnic diversity in the community.

Drawing together leadership teams of diverse cultural origins presents a unique challenge. This will take sensitivity, skill, and commitment. We need cultural sensitivity to navigate relationships and form cohesive groups. We need tact to persuade representatives of the dominant culture to surrender ownership of long-held positions of ministry. Effective communication, and formal and informal training in different styles to match people's expectations, will take persistence and hard work but will result in long-term gains. This begins with the decision that choosing and training leaders will not be politically but missionally driven.

Conclusion

In this chapter, we've seen the concrete outworking of all that has gone before. In short, we've looked at some of the challenging work to be done and changes to be made. I want you to know, fellow pastor, that I know what it takes to choose multiculturalism and lead a congregation to desire multiculturalism.

These changes do not happen quickly. It takes discernment to pinpoint when to pull back and wait, and when to push forward. It takes deep conviction that multiculturalism is God-willed and God-empowered in order to stay the course. The main thing is to persevere, keep learning, keep believing, keep praying, and continue growing.

Based on this chapter, consider . . .

- What small changes can you begin to make to become more visibly inclusive:

  In the space of worship?

  In general atmosphere?

  In the worship service?

- How can you get your congregation to be willing to invest in making changes in favor of multiculturalism?

Getting Started

- Ask yourself: "What stands between my congregation and multicultural growth?" Make a list.
- Pray about this list.
- Ask the Lord to show you one thing on the list to be your starting point.
- Ask him to show you a few people who might be open to change.
- Start informal conversations with these people. Bounce off your ideas. See what happens.
- Keep at it until there are a few people convinced that change is needed.
- Build momentum, and then start asking questions about how we can make change happen.
- Start wooing the opposition.

"The challenge of ethnic, economic and educational diversity in our churches is that we need to understand others, we have to learn to love those who are not like us, and . . . learn to fellowship with, cooperate with, and make decisions with those who are not like us."

—Scot McKnight

Section 3 Summary
Discerning the Opportunities

In this section, we learned
- A multicultural congregation develops organically out of the church's cultural context and its response to community needs.
- Meaningful relationships are means of grace for God's healing love to touch people's lives.
- Congregational life is the space where we concretely demonstrate that the church is a place to belong for all kinds of people together.

Led by the Spirit, compelled by love, we extend our hands and draw others into a place of belonging.

CONCLUSION

▼▲▼

I hope that you are excited about multicultural ministry, that you see it as feasible where you are, with your people, and that you intend to learn more and get into this exciting ministry area.

I have given only a small indication of the "theory" behind multicultural ministry: Demographics. Biblical and Wesleyan foundations.

I encourage you to learn more in each of these areas.

Likewise, literature and media are available to help us develop cultural awareness and communication skills. I've had to navigate many different cultural groups, besides my own, throughout my life. Yet, I feel like a beginner when it comes to clear, sensitive communication. We never stop learning, but we can aim for more learning and growing.

The pastors and practitioners whose thoughts and experiences have brought this handbook to life are your ministry partners—Nazarene leaders across North America. Reach out to them, reach out to your regional multicultural ministry leaders. They can point you to helpful resources.

I pray that you will continue, if you're in the process and begin, if you haven't, and let's follow the fiery cloudy pillar (Exodus 13) into God's tomorrow.

A social or political agenda does not drive our pursuit of multicultural ministry. Instead, we are driven by God-given vision, by biblical and theological mandates.

Developing a multicultural congregation is a process. It takes time to seek God's vision, to share that vision with a congregation, to walk with the congregation toward readiness. It takes time to change. But we do have to start.

Start with the conviction that the Holy Spirit has gone before; he is at work preparing the hearts, conversations, and opportunities for us to move ahead with the individuals, families, and people groups that are waiting for us to *go*.

"A great door for effective work has opened to me, and there are many who oppose me" (1 Cor. 16:9, NIV).

WORKS CITED
▼▲▼

Blackaby, Henry T., and Claude V. King. *Experiencing God*. Nashville: Broadman & Holman Publishers, 2014.

Davis, Ken. "Multicultural Church Planting Models," *The Journal of Ministry and Theology:* Spring 2003.

Dietrich, Andreas. *Discerning Congregational Culture for Pastoral Ministry: The Church Clergy Survey*. Dissertation, Asbury Theological Seminary, 2007. http://place .asburyseminary.edu/ecommonsatsdissertations/284/

Lewis-Giggetts, Tracey M. *The Integrated Church*. Kansas City: Beacon Hill Press of Kansas City, 2011.

Little, Eric. "Where to Begin in Multicultural Ministry." http://www.seedbed.com/ where-to-begin-in-multicultural-ministry/January 31, 2017.

McKnight, Scot. *A Fellowship of Differents: Showing the World God's Design for Life Together*. Grand Rapids, MI: Zondervan Press, 2014.

Plantinga, Cornelius, Jr. "Educating for Shalom," Calvin College, n.d.

Qadeer, Mohammed Abdul. *Multicultural Cities: Toronto, New York, and Los Angeles*. Toronto: University of Toronto Press, 2016.

Rah, Soong-Chan. *Many Colors*. Chicago: Moody Publishers, 2010.

Sheffield, Dan. "Genuine Christianity: Wesleyan Theology and Praxis in a Multicultural Society." Tyndale Wesley Symposium. Toronto, 2014.

Swanson, James. *Dictionary of Biblical Languages with Semantic Domains*. "Hebrew (Old Testament)" electronic ed., HGK132. Oak Harbor: Logos Research Systems, Inc., 1997.

Taber, Charles R. "In the Image of God: The Gospel and Human Rights," *International Bulletin of Missionary Research:* July 2002.

Toegel, Ginka, and Jean-Louis Barsoux, "3 Situations Where Cross-Cultural Communication Breaks Down," *Harvard Business Review*. June 8, 2016. https://hbr.org /2016/06/3-situations-where-cross-cultural-communication-breaks-down.

USA Today, June 11, 2015. http://www.usatoday.com/story/news/2015/06/11/pew -multiracial-survey/71077722/

Whiteman, Darrell L. "The Role of Ethnicity and Culture in Shaping Western Mission Agency Identity," *Missiology*: 34.1.

http://gmdac.iom.int/global-migration-trends-factsheet.

http://www.pewresearch.org/fact-tank/2016/03/31/10-demographic-trends-that-are -shaping-the-u-s-and-the-world/.

http://www.statcan.gc.ca/pub/91-551-x/91-551-x2017001-eng.htm.

http://gmdac.iom.int/global-migration-trends-factsheet.

http://cis.org/Immigrants-in-the-United-States for helpful, up-to-date information about immigrant settlements in the United States.

http://www.pewsocialtrends.org/2013/02/07/second-generation-americans/.

https://www.watershedassociates.com/learning-center-item/direct-communication -vs-indirect-communication.html.

RECOMMENDED READING
▼▲▼

Divided by Faith Building: A Healthy Multi-Ethnic Church Mandate, Commitments and Practices of a Diverse Congregation, Mark DeYmaz, Josey-Bass, 2010.

Emotional Intelligence: Why It Can Matter More Than IQ, Daniel Goleman, Random Book House, 1995.

Evangelical Religion and the Problem of Race in America, Michael Emerson and Christian Smith, Oxford University Press, 2000.

One Body One Spirit—Principles of Successful Multiracial Churches, George A. Yancey, IVP, 2003.

United by Faith: The Multiracial Congregation as an Answer to the Problem of Race. Curtiss Paul Deyoung, Michael O. Emerson, George Yancey, Karen Chai, Oxford University Press, 2003.

The Wolf Shall Dwell with the Lamb: A Spirituality for Leadership in Multicultural Community, Eric H. F. Law, Chalice Press, 1993.

NOTES
▼▲▼

Preface

1. Philip Jenkins, Plenary Speaker, ATS President's Meeting, San Antonio, Tex., Feb. 8, 2015.

2. Ibid.

3. Paul Taylor, *The Next America,* April 10, 2014. Cited 4/5/15, online: http://www.pewresearch.org/next-america/#Immigration-Is-Driving-Our-Demographic-Makeover.

4. Ibid.

5. *Six Seminaries Set Enrollment Records.*

Chapter 1

1. Soong-Chan Rah, *Many Colors* (Chicago: Moody Publishers, 2010), 14.

2. Mohammed Abdul Qadeer, *Multicultural Cities: Toronto, New York, and Los Angeles* (Toronto: University of Toronto Press, 2016), 21.

3. Tracey M. Lewis-Giggetts, *The Integrated Church.* (Kansas City: Beacon Hill Press of Kansas City, 2011), 29.

4. Ken Davis, "Multicultural Church Planting Models," *The Journal of Ministry and Theology*: Spring 2003, 115.

5. http://gmdac.iom.int/global-migration-trends-factsheet.

6. Ibid.

7. http://www.pewresearch.org/fact-tank/2016/03/31/10-demographic-trends-that-are-shaping-the-u-s-and-the-world/.

8. http://www.statcan.gc.ca/pub/91-551-x/91-551-x2017001-eng.htm.

9. Statistics obtained from http://gmdac.iom.int/global-migration-trends-factsheet.

10. See http://cis.org/Immigrants-in-the-United-States for helpful, up-to-date information about immigrant settlements in the United States.

11. http://www.pewsocialtrends.org/2013/02/07/second-generation-americans/.

12. Ibid.

13. Ibid.

14. *USA Today* (June 11, 2015). http://www.usatoday.com/story/news/2015/06/11/pew-multiracial-survey/71077722/.

Chapter 2

1. Both in its physical and cosmic dimensions, diversification points beyond itself to the creative Word (Gen. 1:3, 6, 9, 11, 14, 20, 24, 26) of the one God in three Persons: Father (Ps.

33:6-7; Heb. 1:1-2), Son (John 1:3-5, 10; Col. 1:16; Heb. 1:1-2), and Holy Spirit (Gen. 1:2; Ps. 104:30).

He holds it together (Col. 1:17) and, despite its subjection to the fissures of sin (Rom. 8:19-20), promises to reunite all things in Christ (Rom. 8:21; Eph. 1:10).

The creation is good (Gen. 1:12, 18, 21, 25, especially 31). It is pleasant (Gen. 2:9), individually distinguished (Gen. 1:7, 9-13, 16, 21, 24; 2:1, 9) and relationally compatible (Gen. 2:18, 23-25; 3:8a), a concord that is morally contingent (Gen. 2:16-17).

2. Cornelius Plantinga, Jr., "Educating for Shalom," *Calvin College*, undated, 1: "The webbing together of God, humans, and all creation in justice, fulfillment, and delight is what the Old Testament prophets call shalom. We call it peace, but it means far more than mere peace of mind or cease-fire among enemies. In the Bible shalom means universal flourishing, wholeness, and delight—a rich state of affairs that inspires joyful wonder as its Creator and Savior opens doors and welcomes the creatures in whom he delights."

3. "One can make a claim for universal human rights on the transcendent ground that human beings—*every* human being, *all* human beings—are created in the image and likeness of God and therefore possess an inalienable and innate dignity that no one can rightly take away on any pretext whatever." Victor P. Hamilton, *The Book of Genesis, Chapters 1-17* (Grand Rapids: Eerdmans, 1990), 346.

4. *Ho anthropos* (LXX). "The Hebrew for man (*ādām*, whence "Adam," 2:20) is related to the word for ground (*ădāmâh*; cf. 3:17)." Charles A. Briggs, Francis Brown, S. R. Driver and Richard Whitaker, *The Abridged Brown-Driver-Briggs Hebrew-English Lexicon of the Old Testament: From A Hebrew and English Lexicon of the Old Testament* (Oak Harbor, WA: Logos Research Systems, Inc., 1997, c1906).

5. James Swanson, *Dictionary of Biblical Languages With Semantic Domains: Hebrew (Old Testament)*, electronic ed., HGK132 (Oak Harbor, WA: Logos Research Systems, Inc., 1997).

6. Charles R. Taber, "In the Image of God: The Gospel and Human Rights," *International Bulletin of Missionary Research* (July 2002): 98. He claims, "The Hebrew Scriptures provide the first and most fundamental truth to undergird the concept of human rights: that human beings, male and female, are created in the image and likeness of God and therefore have an inalienable dignity and uniqueness (Gen 1:26–30; Ps 8:4–8)." Citing Kathleen MacArthur, Taber adds that human creation in God's image is "the religious basis for human rights. It is difficult to see how any other basis can possibly support or give meaning to the rights claimed on behalf of humanity" (102).

7. "This family tree tells us that God's blessing to Noah means in reality God's blessing on the whole of subsequent human history. All human people, even of different national and cultural identities—as chapter 10 itself accepts—are of the same origin, have the same dignity, and belong to the same world. This undercuts all human divisiveness based on nationality, culture and race. However good, however rich national and cultural diversity can be, it should never be allowed to cloud the more fundamental fact that all human people share the same nature, breathe the same air, live on the same earth, and owe their life to the same God" (Hamilton, *Genesis 1-17*, 332).

8. Anthropologist Darrell L. Whiteman underscores ethnicity as a reflection of God's creation. In clarifying issues of race he captures the challenge: "To understand how we can celebrate cultural diversity as an expression of God's creation in the body of Christ, without

that diversity degenerating into ethnic rivalries within . . . our churches." Darrell L. White-man, "The Role of Ethnicity and Culture in Shaping Western Mission Agency Identity," *Missiology* 34, No. 1 (Jan. 2006): 59-70.

9. For an analysis of biblical terms describing people groups within "humanity in all of its subdivisions," see Alan Johnson, "Analyzing the Frontier Mission Movement and Unreached People Group Thinking. Part 1: The Frontier Mission Movement's Understanding of the Modern Mission Era," *International Journal of Frontier Missions* 18:2 (Summer 2001): 84.

10. God's providential care reaches beyond Israel across all his works (Ps. 145:9). The family played a protective role, and large families were encouraged in Israel for economic, religious, and social reasons. "The solidarity of a large family was maintained around the father figure" (Geoffrey W. Bromiley, ed., *The International Standard Bible Encyclopedia*, s.v. "Family" [Grand Rapids: Eerdmans, 1982]). For divine providence in general, see Ps. 136:25-26; 147:7-9; Matt. 6:26. The family unit inculcates and regulates human values, see 1 Tim. 3:4-5, 12; Ps. 101:7. Cornelius is one such example (Acts 10:1-2). Households become receptacles of salvation, as in the case of Lydia (Acts 16:14-15), a jailer (Acts 16:31-32), and an official of a synagogue (Acts 18:8).

11. Bromiley, *International Standard Bible Encyclopedia*, s.v. "Family."

12. Hamilton, *Genesis 1-17*, 346.

13. "One can make a claim for universal human rights on the transcendent ground that human beings—*every* human being, *all* human beings—are created in the image and like-ness of God and therefore possess an inalienable and innate dignity that no one can rightly take away on any pretext whatever" (Hamilton, *Genesis 1-17*, 346).

14. Hamilton, *Genesis 1-17*, 332.

15. "This family tree tells us that God's blessing to Noah means in reality God's bless-ing on the whole of subsequent human history. All human people, even of different national and cultural identities—as chapter 10 itself accepts—are of the same origin, have the same dignity, and belong to the same world. This undercuts all human divisiveness based on na-tionality, culture and race. However good, however rich national and cultural diversity can be, it should never be allowed to cloud the more fundamental fact that all human people share the same nature, breathe the same air, live on the same earth, and owe their life to the same God" (Hamilton, *Genesis 1-17*, 332).

Chapter 4

1. Dan Sheffield, "Genuine Christianity: Wesleyan Theology and Praxis in a Multicul-tural Society." Tyndale Wesley Symposium, Toronto, 2014, 2.

2. Ibid., 4.

3. Ibid., 11.

4. Ibid., 9.

5. Ibid.

6. Ibid., 2.

7. Ibid., 8.

8. Ibid., 9.

Chapter 5

1. Rah, *Many Colors*, 38.

2. Ibid.

3. In a 2007 Doctor of Ministry dissertation (Asbury), Andreas Dietrich addresses the question of congregational cultural self-awareness. He reviews cultural models in somewhat greater detail than we have done here and offers a simple, helpful church survey. Something like this can be of immeasurable value to the church's leadership team. "Discerning Congregational Culture for Pastoral Ministries: The Church Culture Survey," http://place.asbury seminary.edu/ecommonsatsdissertations/284/.

4. Unless otherwise indicated, ideas and quotations in this section are taken from Eric Little, "Where to Begin in Multicultural Ministry." http://www.seedbed.com/where-to -begin-in-multicultural-ministry/January 31, 2017.

5. Dietrich, "Discerning Congregational Culture," 138-39.

6. Little, "Where to Begin."

7. Rah, *Many Colors,* 107-8.

Chapter 6

1. Rah, *Many Colors,* 90.

2. Ibid., 91.

3. Ibid..

4. Ibid.

5. https://www.watershedassociates.com/learning-center-item/direct-communication -vs-indirect-communication.html

6. https://www.watershedassociates.com/learning-center-item/task-orientation-vs-re lationship-orientation.html

7. Rah, *Many Colors,* 103.

8. Ibid., 103-4.

9. Ibid., 107.

Chapter 7

1. Ginka Toegel and Jean-Louis Barsoux, "3 Situations Where Cross-Cultural Communication Breaks Down," *Harvard Business Review.* June 8, 2016. https://hbr.org/2016/06 /3-situations-where-cross-cultural-communication-breaks-down.

Chapter 8

1. Henry T. Blackaby and Claude V. King, *Experiencing God* (Nashville: Broadman & Holman Publishers, 1990), 72.

Chapter 9

1. Rah, *Many Colors,* 136.

2. Ibid., 130.

3. Scot McKnight, *A Fellowship of Differents: Showing the World God's Design for Life Together* (Grand Rapids: Zondervan Press, 2014), Kindle ed., loc. 240-291.

4. Rah, *Many Colors,* 166.

5. Ibid., 186

Chapter 10

1. Little, "Where to Begin."